BECHUANALAND

BECHUANALAND

*Pan-African Outpost or
Bantu Homeland?*

a

EDWIN S. MUNGER

*Issued under the auspices of the
Institute of Race Relations, London*

OXFORD UNIVERSITY PRESS

LONDON   NEW YORK

1965

Oxford University Press, Amen House, London E.C.4

GLASGOW   NEW YORK   TORONTO   MELBOURNE   WELLINGTON
BOMBAY   CALCUTTA   MADRAS   KARACHI   LAHORE   DACCA
CAPE TOWN   SALISBURY   NAIROBI   IBADAN   ACCRA
KUALA LUMPUR   HONG KONG

Printed in Great Britain by R. J. Acford Ltd., Chichester

CONTENTS

AUTHOR'S PREFACE

THE field work for this brief account of a corner of modern Africa was possible only through the assistance of the Rockefeller Foundation. The writer is also indebted to the Ford Foundation, the Carnegie Corporation, the Fulbright Program, the Institute of Current World Affairs, and the American Universities Field Staff, for directly and indirectly supporting a dozen previous African field seasons.

Much talk is heard of the truly enormous sums of money to be dispensed by American 'philanthropoids'. But the sums they have available to spend are puny beside the elephantine research tasks and educational programmes to be undertaken. It is only through hard work, unusual insight, and courage to risk misjudgment that foundations are collectively able to be a catalytic force far beyond their financial resources. Their substantial grants to African countries, particularly in the field of higher education, are often in close collaboration with British foundations and governmental departments; when guided by local African leadership foundations offer some of the brightest hopes for a sturdy, economically healthy, and democratic Africa.

The writer is also grateful for the cordial reception and constructive criticisms he received from Her Majesty's Commissioner, Mr. Peter Fawcus, and members of his staff in Bechuanaland. Captain Herbert Bartaune's flights across the country were of immense value. The friendliness of the Bechuana people and of their leaders is much appreciated. Professor I. Schapera, who is without peer in the study of the African life and history of Bechuanaland, made a number of cogent and helpful criticisms. The assistance of Mrs. Gerda Chambers in the preparation and Mrs. Lucille Lozoya in the typing of this manuscript is gratefully acknowledged.

Finally, the opinions expressed in this publication are solely the responsibility of the writer, and are not to be taken as reflecting the views of the Rockefeller Foundation, the Institute of Race Relations, or of any Government.

EDWIN S. MUNGER

California Institute of Technology.

Pasadena, California

June 1964.

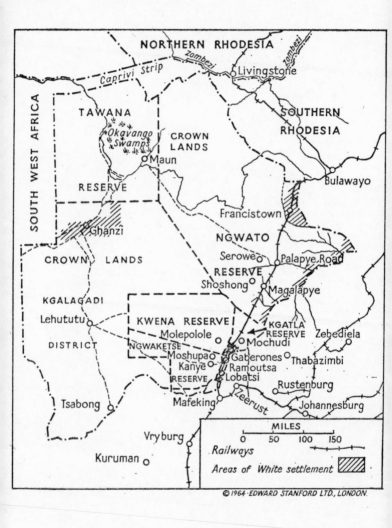

NORTHERN RHODESIA

Zambezi

Caprivi Strip

Livingstone

SOUTHERN RHODESIA

SOUTH WEST AFRICA

TAWANA

Okavango Swamps

CROWN LANDS

Maun

RESERVE

Bulawayo

Ghanzi

Francistown

CROWN LANDS

NGWATO

Serowe

Palapye Road

RESERVE

KGALAGADI

Shoshong

Magalapye

Lehututu

KWENA RESERVE

Molepolole

KGATLA RESERVE

Zebediela

DISTRICT

NGWAKETSE

Moshupa

Kanye

Mochudi

Gaberones

Ramoutsa

Thabazimbi

RESERVE

Lobatsi

Rustenburg

Tsabong

Mafeking

Zeerust

Johannesburg

Vryburg

Kuruman

MILES

0   50   100   150

Railways

Areas of White settlement

© 1964·EDWARD STANFORD LTD., LONDON.

INTRODUCTION

BECHUANALAND, one of the United Kingdom's three High Commission Territories in southern Africa, is not only being born as a nation—it is also becoming a battleground between the ideology and the armed forces of Pan-Africanism on the north, and the racial thinking and military establishment of the Republic of South Africa on the south. Through early 1964, the primary political focus was upon refugees fleeing the Republic; in most instances, simply passing through the Protectorate on their way to Dar es Salaam and points north. But one rather different event to be discussed in detail in this book is the kidnapping of Kenneth Abrahams, a Coloured doctor, inside Bechuanaland, and his subsequent release by the South African Government.

The B.P. (as it is known locally) has 1,400 miles of common frontier with South West Africa. Depending upon World Court decisions and actions in the United Nations, this border is a potentially explosive factor in world politics. Another source of possible political dispute, and of military action, is the proximity of Bechuanaland to southern Angola, separated from it only by the eastern half of the thirty-mile-wide Caprivi Zipfel.

The political future of the three High Commission Territories is a question mark. Only recently did Great Britain cease to have her High Commissioner in Pretoria doubling as the Ambassador to South Africa, and responsible for Basutoland, Swaziland, and Bechuanaland. In addition, Prime Minister Verwoerd's proposal for a referendum in the three territories about association with South Africa hangs in politically-charged air.

We will discuss the Protectorates and South Africa later, because they are far more integral a part of South African Bantu policy than generally realised. A senior South African official put it candidly to the writer: 'We must show that we can work with the emerging African states. If we were to take over Bechuanaland physically, it would make a farce of our whole Bantustan policy.'

Judging from the international and continental pressures involved, the B.P. could simply become a pawn on the African chessboard or, in another common metaphor, ground between the stones of black and white nationalism. But the gestation of a Bechuanaland nation raises the possibility of the people of that country evolving a policy of their own, and of playing a significant role in the affairs of the major African powers.

The words of Seretse Khama to the writer in Lobatsi, B.P., forecast such a development: 'Our role is not one of violence. We will achieve our independence without it. Our mission for Africa will be to demonstrate for our neighbour South Africa that we have a stable African government in which no man is discriminated against on racial grounds and in which the living standards of all are being raised.'

Before expanding on some of the issues just raised, this study sketches the demographic and physical background of Bechuanaland, and traces the significant historical threads leading to contemporary nation-building. It then analyses the attitudes of the diverse inhabitants towards their country and outlines the present and potential economic development. Relations between Bechuanaland and other countries then become meaningful, and lead to some conclusions.

I. PEOPLE AND COUNTRYSIDE

WHAT are the Bechuanas like? Individuals, of course, run the gamut of human experiences, with exceptions to every generalisation. But peoples do have particular characteristics. Yet it is often difficult and misleading to analyse the character of a people while under colonial rule. It seems to stifle some aspects of artistic development and qualities of generosity on one hand, while it certainly puts a damper on excesses which may stem from what westerners would describe as character defects. The variegated individuality of a people is more difficult to observe in an essentially colonial situation—even in a situation such as Bechuanaland, with a history of good race relations and a sympathetic administration.

Henry Lichtenstein travelled through the southernmost part of Bechuana country in 1805 and quotes the views of men he encountered in his journeys. One of these, Van der Lingen, a missionary, refers to the 'perverseness' of the Bechuanas 'who would not receive Christian instruction'. Yet on closer questioning, he conceded his mission predecessors had been driven away because of a 'querulousness and thirst of rule'. Another missionary, John Kok, said the Bechuanas were 'prone to anger, artful, suspicious, and warlike . . .' But if one examines the historical record of European action in their territory, there is much reason for harbouring suspicions and being prone to anger. If Europeans have so long made sweeping generalised statements about African tribes, it is too much to expect that in those days Africans would distinguish what might be a 'good' European from the general run.

A generation later, David Livingstone came to know the Bechuana more intimately. Scattered through his letters (brilliantly edited by Professor I. Schapera) are such comments as (1841): 'The Bechuanas are great beggars.

Indeed they seem to make it a matter of conscience to neglect no opportunity of asking, and a refusal does not by any means put them out if it is done in a jocular way.' But the famous missionary recognised that 'It is only occasionally they think it is worth while to tell you what their opinion of you is, and really it is ludicrous enough to hear their epithets. Instead of getting vexed by them, they always powerfully excite my risible faculties.'

The next year, Livingstone thought: 'There is no goodness among them unless it is implanted by the gospel. I should not be the least surprised to hear of treachery from any of them, they have no fear of God before their eyes.'

Reading early missionary accounts of African peoples is often like listening to a prosecutor in court, who is utterly convinced of his case. Because we almost always lack the defendant's answers—although some long ignored or suppressed ones can be found—the resulting judgment we often form about earlier African societies is at the worst distorted, and at the best sympathetic but lacking in facts.

Granted that the personality of the Bechuanas will be much easier to perceive when they have greater control over their own affairs, they do appear to be a fairly average African cattle people. That is to say, they do not stand out for warlike or aggressive qualities, nor as being particularly meek; they are neither exceptionally hardworking nor lazy. The few who have had educational advantages can hold their own with members of any tribe or nation. But the great mass are so limited in formal education, and so much of what they know best is in the esoteric realm of cattle raising, that to one who would judge by broad African standards, they appear a relatively unexuberant and simple pastoral people. In a Bechuana beerhall, there is little of the colour, excitement, and sense of virility one feels in Nigeria, nor is there among their women the degree of cleverness and drive one finds amongst market women in Accra. And, of course, they lack the sophistication of the urbanised and westernised man who lives in a Johannesburg suburb, even if the man still has tribal rights in the Ciskei. Perhaps because they have far less education, the Bechuanas do not have the quickness or adaptability one delights in with many Nyasas, nor have they the reputation for being able to perform difficult industrial tasks enjoyed by their fellow migrants, the Basuto. On the other hand, one has a feeling of greater openness and ability to develop along modern economic lines than one senses in a Masai *manyatta* (encampment). Many of the Bechuana disadvantages, such as nomadism and its effect on education, are ones they share with other cattle people.

With the exception of an *élite* numbering under 1,000, one can compare the Bechuana people with a potentially fertile but dry field growing mediocre crops. What will happen when water, in the form of broader education, irrigates the field, is impossible to assess. One can say that the present generation is likeable, desirous of learning, and neither filled with hate of another tribe nor of Europeans. Their apparent willingness to accept the formerly despised Bushmen as equal citizens is a hallmark of tolerance.

The Bechuanas' Texas-size (225,000 square miles) arid territory contains about 500,000 to 600,000 people (by recent estimate of the Queen's Commissioner after a pilot census—almost double earlier figures) and 1,325,000 head of cattle. Whereas Texas, with its open plains and cities, averages 28 people per square mile, Bechuanaland has a low-density ratio of only about 2, a major hindrance to development. The population is 99 per cent African, with approximately 3,000 whites, 1,000 Euro-Africans, and 250 Asians. As far back as 1921, there were 1,700 whites against an estimated 150,000 Africans. Although the percentage of Europeans is insignificant, they are mostly settled along the line of rail in the best watered part of eastern Bechuanaland, and have been responsible for the development of nearly all the commercial enterprises. The Bechuana are also concentrated mainly in the eastern part of the territory.

The largest towns are Kanye, with approximately 30,000 Africans, and Serowe, with 16,000 Africans. Francistown has the largest number of Europeans (1,000), and is the main commercial centre, now being rivalled by Lobatsi, which is also the temporary legislative capital and site of the slaughterhouse. Other towns along the eastern line of rail southward are Papaye, Mahalapye and the future capital, Gaberones.

Among the lands where Europeans have settled are the Lobatsi, Gaberones and Tuli blocks in the east, where the chiefs ceded land in connection with the railway in 1895, and the Tati Concession on the north-east border with Southern Rhodesia. European farmers also have land rights in the far west Ghanzi settlement under an agreement engineered by Cecil Rhodes in 1899 and extended by the Bechuanaland Government in 1959. It is against these somewhat loose arrangements that the gestation of Bechuanaland nation-building must be considered.

Bechuanaland takes its name from many closely-related Bantu tribes known collectively as the Bechuana, and all speaking Sechuana or, in an alternative spelling, Tswana. Among the tribal territories, the Bamangwato is the largest (44,941 square miles), and has about one-third of the total population. The next largest are the Bakwena, Bangwaketse, and Batawana territories. Ethnically, the African population is more heterogeneous than that of the other two High Commission Territories. The tribal territories are all held by subdivisions of the most important tribal group— the Bechuanas—most of whom entered the territory from the Transvaal in the first half of the 18th century.

Bakgatla people live on both sides of the Transvaal border, but have separate chiefs, although the Bakgatla chief in the B.P. claims over-all rule. A majority of the Barolong actually live in the Republic of South Africa, and the tribal head-quarters has long been Mafeking, on the Republican side of the border. Other Bantu groups include Koba from Northern Rhodesia, Herero from South West Africa, some

Southern Rhodesian peoples, and the long-resident Kgala-gadi. The Bushmen are primarily significant ethnologically. Almost all of the non-Bechuana Africans are under the tribal control, not always happily, of the Bechuana chiefs.

Physical Geography

The lives of the people of the territory are closely inter-woven with their physical surroundings. To understand them, one must begin with the underlying geology.

Beneath the surface of the territory is a huge depression in the basement rock which has been filling with sediment and volcanic ash since pre-Cambrian times. On top of this, varying from 300 feet in the north to 100 feet in the south, are the Kalahari sands. On the east, substantial areas of exposed schists and sedimentary rocks form a complex pattern. Likely mineral finds include hematite, gold, nickel, copper, and diamonds, but so far 90 per cent of the limited mineral production has been asbestos. Seams of medium quality coal have been found.

The territory, at an average elevation of 3,300 feet, is exceptionally flat, and 84 per cent is covered by sparse grass and a thornbush savannah. However, dunes occur only in the extreme southwest, and it is erroneous to describe Bechuanaland as a desert. The rainfall is only about 18 inches a year, with a maximum around 27 inches in the north, down to under 10 inches in the Kalahari. Rain which does come falls in the summer between October and April. The lack of running water and of underground supplies derives, in part, from the fine texture of the sands. These hold the limited precipitation near the surface and provide moisture for long periods. The climate is sub-tropical, moderated by the elevation and low humidity. Winter nights are cool with occasional frost, and the hot summers are tempered by a prevailing north-east breeze in the late evening.

There are hills in the north, east, and west, and water courses are formed in the better rains. At various periods in the past, the rainfall was much heavier, and a whole ancient river system can be seen in the landscape. In this fossil system of a thousand years ago or more, the Molopo and Nossob Rivers, now rarely holding water, cut their way hundreds of feet below the plain. Water, then, is the chief factor limiting economic growth today. Permanent water is found only in the Okavango River and its huge swamps in the northwest. Later we will discuss the studies of its flow, now largely lost through evaporation and transpiration, which might be used both for irrigation near the present swamps, channelled in canals, or put into existing dry river systems.

Soils in the less sandy parts of the territory are not very fertile, but in the Tuli block and the Tati concession they would support excellent crops with a high return if they had water. However, experienced scientists have warned against allowing inexpert European or African cattle men to graze large parts of the Kalahari, lest a delicately balanced equilibrium of nature be destroyed for hundreds of years by even moderately heavy browsing.

Kalahari Desert

The Kalahari is the most famous and dominant physical feature of the B.P., yet it is subject to wide misunderstanding. It is substantially a desert if one means deserted by people. It does have some sand dunes in the south-west, but very little of it would be usable in a Hollywood 'Beau Geste' film. Adequate vegetation to support wild animals and even domesticated cattle is found in nearly all parts of the Kalahari. Criss-crossing it recently by small plane at 100 feet elevation, I circled a lone giraffe in the centre of a huge salt pan in what was almost the geographical dead centre of the Kalahari. But he did not appear weak, and grazing was available a few miles on. Actually, as one drives westwards across the Kalahari from Lobatsi to Ghanzi, the land becomes distinctly drier on approaching Ghanzi. But it is here that the cattle population builds up, and some farmers have grown wealthy on their livestock.

The key to the Kalahari being a desert is not sand or lack of vegetation, but lack of surface water. The gemsbuck and other game survive in their tens of thousands because of an ability to lick up the dew and to extract liquids from what they eat. The nomadic Bushmen are famed for their use of the tsamma melon. It contains liquid, and slakes the thirst of the Bushmen, but it is not recommended for westernised stomachs, short of deathly thirst. It is more akin to drinking very bitter lemon juice than to the usual breakfast melon. The Bushmen are also known for their unique ability to suck up water from a damp piece of ground by inserting a straw. They transfer mouthfuls of water to gourds and will generously offer it to a stranger.

Ghanzi survives as a farming area in one of the drier parts of the Kalahari because of the presence of a limestone ridge and water lying as close as fifty feet below the surface. In most parts of the Kalahari, given deep water, one could establish cattle stations with a higher carrying capacity than some parts of Arizona or the Australian outback, where cattle are run.

Thus, the image of the Kalahari as a barren waste is erroneous, a conclusion that visiting scientists have been reaching every decade since 1890. It is the 'great thirstland'. The innumerable stories of man and beast dying for lack of water, and of the maddening rush of oxen hot on the scent of water ahead after days in the Kalahari, were true, just as they were true for much of the Great American Desert in the western United States. To drive cattle from Ghanzi 400 miles to the Lobatsi Abattoir is still a hard task fraught with potential danger. Men are occasionally mauled by lions, and those who venture off the regular routes risk death by thirst. But one can already see the hand of man taming this vast waterless expanse.

II. GESTATION OF A NATION

WHAT territorial unity the B.P. (Bechuanaland Protectorate) does possess is due, as much as any single factor, to Khama III, a remarkable individual leader, who became chief of the Bamangwato in 1872. The previous fifty years had been disastrous for his group and for Bechuana groups generally. Not only had many of them been pushed out of the Transvaal by the forces set in motion by *impis* (regiments) of Shaka Zulu; they were often raided by the Zulu breakaways under Mzilikazi, the tribe now known as the Matabele in Southern Rhodesia. But a major weakness was the internal dissension of the Tswana groups. In 1820, Robert Moffat of the London Missionary Society established a post at Kuruman, but his assistance brought peace to only a small area. A broader peace followed when Chief Khama III organised military forces sufficient to deter Mzilikazi's successor, Lobengula, from attacking the stronger Bechuana groups. Khama III was a staunch Christian and virtually prohibited alcohol. As a strong administrator, he further reorganised the tribal life his father had begun to knit together, as had the chiefs of other shattered tribes.

Britain has guaranteed Bechuanaland's territorial integrity for many decades now. However, one must recall that around 1884 one of the Barolong chiefs, Montshiwa, pleaded in vain for promised protection. Groups of Boer 'freebooters' from the Transvaal kept moving into his lands, stopping and searching travellers, ploughing fields, and threatening to use cannon bought in Pretoria against anyone who interfered. The Transvaal Republic was clearly on the side of the Boers outside its borders, and of a group of Bechuana allies. Britain struggled ineffectually to help protect the pro-British Bechuana chiefs from encroachment.

These were the days of the Republic of Stellaland, centred on Vryburg, and north of it the biblically-inspired 'Land of Goshen'. In a series of compromises, the Bechuana tribes lost the great part of what would be the most productive part of their lands, and the border moved northwards. What had been the British Crown Colony of British Bechuanaland since 1885—that is, south of the present-day border at the Molopo River plus the Stellaland and Goshen Republics—became part of the Cape Colony. As a result, the Barolongs are split by the southern B.P. border, and the chief actually lives in South Africa. What the Bechuanas gained—perhaps salvaged is a better description—was a full 'Protectorate' status from Her Majesty's Government which has stood the test of time.

The resolution of the struggle over what was once Bechuanaland involved, first of all, the clash between Paul Kruger's South African Republic (Transvaal) and Cecil Rhodes' Cape Colony. Not only did Rhodes want northern Bechuanaland, but he wanted access to it and to the Rhodesias for trade and missionaries by outflanking the Transvaal on the east. Although J. G. van Niekerk, in setting up Stellaland, had a soundly organised and potentially properous country, its strategic position led to growing pressure. Van Niekerk arranged to join with Goshen and to seek protection from the Transvaal.

Intervention by newly colonial-minded Germany tipped the scales toward a vigorous and successful push by Great Britain and complicated political geography in southern Africa. In 1884, Germany proclaimed its protectorate over the Namaqua-Damaraland coast. The European powers were jockeying for position and trading claims in most parts of Africa. The threat presented to Britain was the linking-up of the Germans in South West Africa with their Boer friends in the South African Republic. Plans were made for a railroad east from Luderitz. Cecil Rhodes saw this political bond as a permanent barrier to the north of the Cape, but it was rivalry in the broader continental sphere which stiffened the British spine. Meanwhile Germany gained substantially in Togo, Cameroons, as well as elsewhere.

British concern for Bechuanaland as part of a power struggle led to a commitment to the British South Africa Company that it could veto any east–west German railway crossing Bechuanaland.

Subsequent rail competition led to the creation of the Caprivi Zipfel north of Bechuanaland from South West Africa to the Rhodesias. This long appendage now looks anachronistic on the modern map of Africa, not unlike an unneeded appendix, but at the time it was crucial to German plans to cross Africa by rail from east to west. After decades of manoeuvering, Germany failed to cross Africa, and Rhodes' dream of an all-British route from south to north did not come true.

The Caprivi Strip is about 30 miles in width and 300 miles long, and is named for Count Caprivi, the German Chancellor and successor to Bismarck. Its creation formed part of the Anglo-German Convention of 1890. This included the cession to Germany of Heligoland, and a number of African agreements involving the Volta River, Togoland, Cameroons, the East African coast, and British protection of Zanzibar. The Caprivi Strip gave Germany access to the upper reaches of the Zambezi, and thus potential but never realised trade routes in central Africa. Its strategic significance was never appreciated in the last century. It is difficult of access and consists mostly of swamp, flooded river, and a few islands towards its apex, where the Zambesi and Chobe Rivers converge. It is administered directly from the Republic of South Africa, separately from South West Africa, of which it is actually a part. It is possible that the Zipfel's long borders with both Angola and Bechuanaland will play an important role as political pressures increase in this part of Africa.

To return to Bechuanaland, once Britain had thwarted the South African Republic and the Germans it was by no means certain that Bechuanaland would remain a separate territory. Lord de Villiers, President of the National Convention, wrote to General Smuts in 1908, five weeks before the Convention in Durban, and suggested giving all of Bechuanaland to the Transvaal. But, despite the widely held assumption that Bechuanaland, Swaziland, and Basutoland would have been handed over in due course to South Africa, Britain resisted demands for doing so immediately. The historian Eric Walker believes that unless it had been understood that the Territories would eventually be transferred, Britain would have refused union in 1910. The history of these relationships is outlined in greater detail by Lord Hailey in his *The Republic of South Africa and the High Commission Territories* (Oxford University Press, 1963).

From this historical sketch it is clear that Bechuanaland's strategic position in the political battleground of southern Africa today is a continuation of a century-old role, but with two main differences. The first of these is that no longer do European states propose and dispose with new African countries, and the second, that never before have the Bechuanas been in a position to affect the outcome. The emergence of modern Bechuana leadership, albeit often with traditional charismatic overtones, marks a new phase in Bechuanaland history.

Seretse Khama's marriage

Probably the key figure in the B.P. today is Seretse Khama. We shall come later to his political role, but now our historical survey would be incomplete without reference to the political difficulties which arose from his marriage in September 1948 to Miss Ruth Williams. Seretse Khama was heir to the Bamangwato Chieftainship, and a law student at the Inner Temple in London. His academic career began in tribal schools and went on in South African institutions to a B.A. While at Oxford, he was chosen to play rugby (under a South African captain) for Balliol.

Ruth Williams had a middle class background, four years in the Women's Auxiliary Air Force and, at the time of her marriage, was a confidential clerk to an underwriter at

Lloyds. One mentions this because the label 'London typist', with implications of little education, social status and responsibility, was unfairly pinned on her in contemporary Press accounts.

The Regent of the Bamangwato at the time was Tshekedi Khama, who had ruled for twenty-three years. He was strongly against the marriage. An intelligent and able man of tremendous drive, and a real autocrat, Tshekedi was Seretse's uncle. However, he had been *in loco parentis* for many years, and was normally addressed as 'father' by Seretse. When Tshekedi was married in 1936, his fifteen-year-old nephew, Seretse, was the best man.

In 1933, Tshekedi tried a white man for an offence against an African. Under statutes dating back to 1891, neither Tshekedi nor any other chief with judicial power had the right to try any white man. The man in question was none-too-savoury a character, and the Regent had strong moral justification. This was a *cause célèbre* for southern Africa of this period and roused strong emotions among Europeans and, indeed, many Africans who wanted a change. The British Government, even if sympathetic with Tshekedi in this particular case, felt it could not accept such a flouting of regulations. Tshekedi displayed his iron determination and refused to follow British wishes. Finally, the acting High Commissioner, Vice-Admiral Evans, called for 200 marines and sailors from a British warship in Cape Town, and marched this naval force across the sand to Serowe to enforce Britain's will upon Tshekedi.

In his resolute fight against the marriage in 1948, Tshekedi brought pressure on Seretse through the British Government and the London Missionary Society, and through a barrage of cables putting forth his own objections and also reflecting an undetermined amount of tribal feeling. Tshekedi's initial success was simply to block a religious wedding when successive Anglican clergy got cold feet under pressure from superiors, but this did not stop the civil marriage. It was the first round in what Sir Winston Churchill described in the

House of Commons as 'a very disreputable transaction'. His specific criticism was of Tshekedi's banishment, but it might apply to the whole series of episodes.

Considerable wrath was directed at a manoeuvre through which Seretse Khama and his wife were invited to London from Bechuanaland, where they had gone to live while the question of the chieftainship was thrashed out. Ruth Khama refused to go lest Seretse somehow be forced to choose between his tribe and his wife. Her suspicions seemed well-grounded when she received a cable from Seretse in London: 'Tribe and myself tricked by British Government stop Am banned from whole Protectorate stop Love Seretse'.

Without recapitulating a long hearing at Lobatsi, starring Tshekedi Khama, a fight between Bamangwato tribesmen and the police in the *kgotla* (meeting place) in which three African police were killed and twelve injured, and various manoeuvres to keep Seretse and Ruth Khama apart, the upshot was that the Khamas eventually settled in Addiscombe, Croydon, for a lengthy stay. The tribe was governed by Rasebolai Kgamane, an experienced soldier, as head of the African Authority. An Order in Council declared 'that neither Seretse Khama nor Tshekedi Khama nor their children shall hereafter be eligible to be chief, or acting chief, or regent of the tribe, or to be a member of a council of regency of the tribe, or to summon the tribe in *kgotla* for any purpose, or to preside or exercise any of the functions of the president of any *kgotla* of the tribe'. The same policy was envisaged by the Conservative Government which succeeded Labour and which did not at the time lift the ban on the Khamas. It is probably true that no official written representations were ever made by South Africa. However, the writer accepts the views of responsible members of both British parties that at the time the possible repercussions from South Africa about the inter-racial marriage did weigh heavily with the British Government.

A great deal of water has subsequently flowed down the Zambesi. In many ways, the National Party Government in South Africa has matured in office and with the confidence of three successive victories at the polls, and it seems that a less rigid stand is taken on such matters as inter-racial liaisons. Even internally, the Immorality Act, which tragically caught in its clutches so many men including some prominent in public life, was not so stringently enforced by 1963. This is not easily proved but it is the writer's considered opinion that a tacit agreement now prevails to go slow on attempting to uncover, and to prosecute, any except flagrant cases. There has been a marked drop in the number of cases mentioned in the Press.

We will discuss subsequently relations between South Africa and the B.P., but suffice it to say that given a similar case today, British action would be much less—if at all—influenced by South African views.

And what are the views of people in Bechuanaland with the passage of time and the death, in 1959, of Tshekedi? Among the Bamangwato, Seretse Khama, long since back in his home in Serowe, has almost all the charismatic attraction he would have as chief. He has the political advantages of (1) not being bothered with the many time-consuming duties of a chief, (2) not being forced to make petty decisions which might create animosity against him in the tribe, and (3) being accepted by most of the chiefs of the B.P. as virtually a chief with strong political backing and without losing the common touch he may need to compete with the Bechuanaland People's Party. He can disavow rigidly traditionalist decisions by chiefs without being disloyal to chieftainship.

In late 1963 it was announced that Rasebolai wished to retire after ten years of valuable service. It was agreed that the eldest son of Tshekedi Khama, Leapeetswe Khama, should be appointed head of the African Authority replacing Rasebolai Kgamane, and the change was made at a *kgotla* in January 1964. The suspension of the Chieftainship was continued, but it was specifically stated by the Government that in view of the wishes of the tribe, Seretse Khama's sons were not excluded from the Chieftainship when they came of age. This means that sporadic criticism of the Khama sons on the racial grounds that they are only 'half-African' has been overcome.

Ruth Khama has gained wide respect from the Bamangwato. Her handling of many traditional roles has solidified her position with some traditionalists. The tribe know her as a person and not as a 'white woman', and they like her. Among the Bamangwato tribesmen, there is a growing sentiment that the Khamas' eldest boy—now away at a formerly all-European school in Bulawayo—should some-day become chief. Opposition might also be strong, but the tide has turned in favour of the Khamas. While they have established themselves personally, what is more important is the westernisation of the Bamangwato Reserve and the B.P. generally. In the sixteen years since the dispute broke out, the Bechuana in general have become more sophisticated. Seretse used to stand out because of his European dress and habits. Now he looks like many an African standing alongside him at a cocktail bar, except for better tailoring. What African racialism there may have been directed against Ruth Khama has lessened in the B.P., despite a greater consciousness of racial conflict elsewhere and the rise of nationalism.

And what of the Europeans in the B.P.? Seretse Khama is downright popular. British sportsmen speak of his sense of humour on the cricket field, and administrators of his common sense. He is a friend and confidant of European officials. Afrikaner farmers spoke warmly of him to me. They stood up and cheered at a political meeting where he explained his views. His sense of humour does as much as anything to endear him to Europeans. Some of his humorous comments—even poking fun at himself—would sound odd in Britain, but they are appreciated in the B.P. A second factor commented on by many Europeans is a complete lack of bitterness, as far as his casual friends could see. One or two British officials—a new generation in the higher posts—have a sense of guilt over the past, but as they were not higher-ups then, they do not find this a barrier. Europeans with strong racial prejudice still live in the B.P., but even in this group Seretse Khama is held in high respect and even esteem. Curiously, one factor cited by several Europeans who are anti-African, but favour Seretse, is his devotion to his wife.

Ruth Khama has had a hard row to hoe with many official wives as well as with the white women generally in the Protectorate. Her own sense of dignity and good manners, and her obvious devotion to her husband and children, have been the major factors in her genuine acceptance by the wives of British officials. They had no alternative but to accept her outwardly, but Mrs. Khama herself gained the inward approval. This issue always seems one-sided. By what right are 'they' judging her, whoever 'they' may be? A more important question, perhaps, is whether she, as the wife of the most influential African leader, is willing to accept 'them'. However, one must also note that in non-official white circles, Mrs. Khama is respected. Among Afrikaner women, respect was summed up in one remark by a more or less typical *huisvrou* (house-wife): 'Well, you know what we think about things like that, but you know I saw her at the Francistown show last month and she is an awfully nice person.'

Although Seretse Khama is still prohibited in South Africa, his marriage is far from a public issue. Indeed, his plane was diverted once during 1963, and he landed at Jan Smuts Airport. Calls to various ministries revealed no antagonism, but some confusion about what to do. In the end, Seretse Khama had lunch at the British High Commission in Pretoria, and motored back to Bechuanaland. This incident was never discussed in the Press and had no repercussions.

To sum up in common phrases which reveal a certain racialism in European languages, in a decade in Bechuanaland Seretse Khama had changed from the *bête noire* of whites and, indeed, of South Africans, to their 'white hope' for moderate, economically progressive African rule.

From Non-Incorporation to Political Parties

Until 1948, when the National Party came to power in South Africa, it was widely assumed that Bechuanaland would be incorporated into the then Union of South Africa. One can summarise an involved legal history by saying that at the founding of a Union of South Africa in 1910, it seemed only a matter of time until the incorporation provided for took place. Indeed, throughout the 1930s, Prime Minister J. B. M. Hertzog pressed in various ways for the final incorporation. This has not taken place because the inhabitants of none of the three territories have ever seemed willing to be incorporated. No British Government would or will hand over the territories to South Africa against the will of the inhabitants. The image created by the National Party since 1948 has killed the prospect of incorporation.

A second event from which to date an incipient Bechuanaland sense of nationhood was economic. As mentioned, until 1956 this desperately poor territory was financially on its own. The British Government asked itself the rhetorical question: 'Why spend British taxpayers' money to build up a territory someone else is going to take over?' But by the late 1950s, the contrast between the virtual void in public services for Bechuanaland and the appalling state of African education, roads, health services, etc., compared with the relatively superior provisions for Africans within the Union of South Africa, had not only drawn a large percentage of the ablest Bechuanas across the border to South Africa, but made the rural slum of Bechuanaland a poor platform from which to criticise the Union. If incorporation was out, then Britain would be judged guilty of appalling neglect of her self-designated colonial responsibilities. It was from these motives that the U.K. Treasury finally gave a modest transfusion to the anaemic Bechuanaland budget.

Although incorporation was no longer a prospect after 1948, it was not until a third key date, Sharpeville in 1960, that all informed people in the Bechuanaland Protectorate finally concluded that incorporation was out of the question.

While blood had begun to flow in the financial arteries of the B.P., the events triggered by the shooting at Sharpeville led to stronger measures against African nationalist groups in South Africa and, in turn, to a steady stream of refugees across the boundary to Bechuanaland. Between 1960 and 1964, the number totalled some 1,400. The B.P. has had far more South African refugees than Swaziland or Basutoland. The refugee route north from Lobatsi to Francistown and on to Tanganyika has become fairly routine, while an easy outlet from the other High Commission Territories is still not available.

The refugees as a group played the decisive role in the beginning of indigenous political movements in the B.P. from 1960 onwards. Not that refugees played a major role themselves, but through numerous contacts and discussions with them, local Bechuanas developed the Bechuanaland People's Party (B.P.P.). Of course, then as now, analysis of refugees by the Bechuanaland Government suggests that only a small percentage of 'refugees' flee for genuine political reasons; many are merely seeking escape from dissatisfactions or complications in their personal life, and try to take advantage of the political asylum offered. This type of refugee created a bad name in the B.P. as in Tanganyika. Likewise, some of the white Communists, most of whom did not reach the B.P. until 1963, antagonised even the most militant Bechuanas with a callous disregard of the B.P.'s best interests.

Under stimulus from Africans of the Republic of South Africa and encouraged by a little more money moving in the territory, various Bechuana groups came rapidly to conceive of their country as a potential nation. Following a year after the Bechuanaland People's Party was the Bechuanaland Democratic Party (B.D.P.). Led by Seretse Khama, it is probably the most popular party in the B.P. today. Both of these parties have effectively preached a B.P. nationalism. I tested this one time in remote Ngamiland by talking with a group of illiterate and barely literate B.P.P. supporters in Maun. They preached equality of all within the B.P. I wondered about the Bushmen (*Masarwa*[1] to the Bechuana), who have been treated as little more than animals by most of the Bantu. 'Do you mean to tell me that the Masarwa can go to school with your children, become officials, and even marry into your family?' The men addressed hesitated and swallowed, until one said: 'eh . . . eh . . . Yes, they are people just like the rest of us, and everyone in the B.P. must be fair men.' This and many other encounters convince me that the two parties have been extraordinarily successful in overcoming traditional antagonisms and building towards a B.P. citizenship. To be sure, there will be bitter Bushman–Bantu rivalries and faction fights among the Bechuana tribes. But these will not approach the bitterness of tribal antagonisms in, say, the Congo or Kenya.

The organisation of political parties is no idle exercise, because the fruits of office are there for the winning. Some African political party will have substantial control of the internal affairs of Bechuanaland before the end of 1965. Such control could be greater than what is now envisaged, and come sooner.

Bechuanaland People's Party

The first political party to be organised (in 1961 for practical purposes) was the Bechuanaland People's Party. The nominal leader is K. T. Motsete. He was a man of

---

[1] Technically a particular tribe of Bushmen with some Bantu admixture. The Masarwa attach themselves to Bechuana cattle owners in a serf-and-master arrangement.

considerable promise when, following secondary schooling in South Africa, he went to London with the assistance of the Carnegie Corporation and took a series of degrees in the early 1930s. Motsete is respected in Bechuanaland as a man of learning, but a fair assessment is that he has never lived up to his promise. He has great personal charm; however, he seems sometimes to lack intellectual sharpness, and, indeed, political acumen. When I asked him how the B.P.P. differed from the Bechuanaland Democratic Party, he replied, 'Well, we aren't really very different,' an answer which would never satisfy his vigorous lieutenants. He is an amiable figurehead, and by nature more of a B.D.P. man.

The driving force in the party is Vice-Chairman Matante. I talked with him in his Francistown home shortly after his return from Moscow. His visit there was something of a mystery because Matante has always followed a strong anti-Communist line, even when an expression of such views seemed irrelevant. Actually, it seems that the whole visit was a colossal mistake: someone else, a woman with a similar name, had been invited to an international women's gathering in Moscow. Thus, no one was prepared for the dynamic leader of the B.P.P. According to Matante, he did not see any of the key people in Moscow who are concerned with Africa, and did not even talk freely with African students at Patrice Lumumba University. He visited it and saw a few buildings and talked with one African student through an interpreter. Some effort was made by members of the Afro-Asian Solidarity Committee to brighten his visit, but it was a dreary mistake.

The apparent Soviet assessment of Matante is understandable. He is far from the class of leaders elsewhere in Africa. One can easily be in error, but I did not feel he had the qualities for success which such present-day leaders as Nkrumah, Mboya and Nyerere had in the days when they were first organising anti-colonial parties. Nevertheless, Matante is superb on the soapbox, and has a shrewdness which stands out in Bechuanaland.

It is interesting to compare him and Mburumba Kerina, the South West Africa leader. Both Kerina and his handsome wife from Los Angeles, and their American-born children, were staying with Matante when I visited him. Kerina has a wide grasp of the political spectrum. On the other hand, Matante seemed unable to sort out the relative strengths in America of the Black Muslims, Lawson's African Nationalists, and the 'Back to Africa' movement within the whole Negro protest movement, appearing to believe that the 'Back to Africa' movement was one of the strongest.

At the present time, it is difficult to assess the strength of breakaway B.P.P. leader Mpho. His political views are to the left of Matante; he is a vigorous personality. His following is now limited, but this could change in a matter of weeks. In general, the Mpho splinter section has associated itself with the African National Congress, whereas the Matante segment has been closer to the Pan-Africanist Congress.

The B.P.P. is poor. Money from Ghana for a Land Rover and loudspeaker equipment was a significant factor in its initial success. Now there is squabbling over the dispersal of the limited Ghanaian funds and a general state of executive uncertainty. Nothing like the close comradeship of the early C.P.P. in Ghana exists. The comparatively small but most politically conscious urban population, particularly the poor and unemployed, are for the B.P.P. Waiters in the Francistown hotels spoke unanimously for the B.P.P. as the 'poor man's party' against the 'rich men'. In a Francistown African beer hall, I found no supporters of the B.D.P., although, if there were a few, they may have feared intimidation. The B.P.P. would probably sweep an election slate in Francistown, Lobatsi, and some of the smaller towns.

The mercurial nature of Bechuanaland politics may mean that whole parties die and new ones are born in a matter of months. President Motsete and Vice-President Matante have argued vigorously in private, and have even ventilated ill feelings in the pages of the Mafeking *Mail* (August 1963). Granted the role of charisma in B.P. politics, and the political leverage of small sums of money, new leaders may be expected to rise rapidly from the ranks.

Bechuanaland Democratic Party

This party also believes in 'one man, one vote'. It did not stand with the B.P.P. for independence in 1964, but rather 'as soon as possible'. It is the party of political moderation and, somewhat, of the 'haves'—those Africans who have education or wealth or traditional authority. In most African situations, the teachers, traders, and chiefs are outvoted by the mass, but not always: not, for instance, in northern Nigeria, another cattle-owning part of Africa.

B.D.P. leader Seretse Khama is a man of outstanding ability. There is a mantle around him from his famous grandfather, Chief Khama, and from his even more able, if hard-headed, uncle, Tshekedi Khama, with whom Seretse had so bitter a struggle. As we have seen Seretse is not the chief of his tribe, and although it is likely that the British would withdraw the bar to this if asked, he is probably too wise to accept the chieftainship. He is one of the most progressive men in Bechuanaland, and is popular with African teachers and businessmen. As such, he regularly clashes with the chiefs in African Council and in the legislature. When it comes to voting in a general election, however, Seretse Khama could certainly count upon the support of the chiefs and upon the many thousands of tribesmen who will take their cues from their traditional leaders. For some chiefs with whom Seretse clashes, he is obviously the 'least bad' candidate for Prime Minister. His birth, experience and sense of responsible leadership make him attractive to the traditionalists.

But it would be a mistake to assume that Seretse Khama is the most active politician in the Democratic Party. That description fits his highly intelligent and effective No. 2

man, Quett Masire. It is Masire who has visited Kenya, Ethiopia, Ghana and elsewhere for political discussions with African leaders. I attended a three-day meeting of the African Council in Lobatsi, and the best and most cogent speeches were made by Quett Masire, a man in his early thirties, and thus junior to most of the members. John Banda, Parliamentary Secretary for Education in Northern Rhodesia, describes Masire: 'He was the brightest boy in our class in South Africa, and we all expected him to be a brilliant scholar.'

Masire is a member of Chief Bathoen's Bankwaketse tribe. Bathoen is the strongest chief among his peers and has often clashed with the young progressives such as Masire. At one stage, he stripped Masire of most of his land and rights, and tried to banish him to a distant part of the reserve. Pressure from Seretse Khama and the British Government smoothed this over. Bathoen is far from completely reactionary towards change, and is proud that at Kanye he has the cleanest town in the B.P. and the best hospital. For a time, Bathoen and his fellow chiefs stayed away from modern politics and used their considerable powers to run affairs their own way. They are somewhat scared now, and form the right wing of the B.D.P., although clashes continue with Seretse Khama over the pace at which tribal traditions should be adjusted to modern conditions. Khama, Masire, and Bathoen are all key figures in the Bechuanaland Legislature.

Attitude of the B.P. Administration

In addition to having probably a slight majority of African support in the B.P., and having the support of nearly all European, Indian, and Coloured residents, the Bechuanaland Democratic Party is the clear favourite of the British Administration. However, one must immediately express the conviction that election procedures and ballot counting will be scrupulously fair, and that if the B.P.P. can muster majority support, it will take over the Government.

The British Government might have wished to advance the probable date of internal African rule to earlier than late 1965, but for various technical reasons such as census, delimitation, the new capital, and other considerations, it could not do so. Some observers see an early election as favouring the chances of the now surging B.D.P., but no favouritism on the part of Her Majesty's Government can be seen.

European Re-orientation

African attitudes and goals are the major key to creating a Bechuanaland nation, but the Europeans, although small in number, also exercise a significant role in nation-building. Perhaps because they had a deeper sense of modern political units, the growth of a B.P. nationalism has been more marked among Europeans than among the vast majority of tribally-oriented Bechuanas.

Until three years ago, European farmers and businessmen looked outward to some other political unit with which they felt a kinship. This was strongest in the isolated Ghanzi block, four hundred miles of terrible road from Lobatsi, across the Kalahari thirstland to the western border of the B.P. The Ghanzi farmers, mostly of Afrikaans origin, had their links across the border to Gobabis in South West Africa. Their mail and supplies came from there. They sent their cream and cattle there for sale. Their children still attend boarding school in South West Africa or in South Africa. On the whole, I find from interviewing numerous farmers in the Ghanzi block that their allegiance is now evenly divided. Cream still goes to Gobabis, but cattle are trekked for up to two weeks to the Lobatsi abattoir. Mail is from the B.P. The new Bechuanaland Safaris' weekly air service has brought a marked psychological change of attitude. Ghanzi has no doctor for hundreds of miles, so when a man had his arm pulled out of the shoulder by a machine, he waited a day and then flew two hours to Lobatsi. In another case, a man who had lost a leg to a lion was flown to Francistown for treatment. Previously, injured people went to South West Africa.

In 1898, Cecil John Rhodes granted 37 farms to Afrikaner farmers in the Ghanzi block. Not many of the original families are still there, and only a few of the Angolan 'trek boers' who returned from their self-imposed exile in Portuguese territory to settle at Ghanzi. They are not happy about social integration. Although apprehensive, there are others among the three hundred Afrikaner farmers and a handful of English-speakers who are willing to think in terms of a Bechuanaland nation. They are not in a region of heavy African population, and have pioneered the country with the help of partially detribalised Bushmen. They talk more wistfully than practically of joining with South West Africa. Actually, their small numbers and isolation from the centres of influence in Bechuanaland work against their carrying much weight with the authorities or the authorities doing very much to them, be authority British or African. However, they were the only European group to resist school integration fully, and, in defiance, sent some fifty children to school out of Bechuanaland.

If Ghanzi Europeans are now partially oriented towards Bechuanaland, the farmers in the Tuli and Gaberones blocks on the eastern border have also begun even more to look inward to Bechuanaland instead of exclusively outward to the Transvaal. While there are close family ties with the Republic, almost every farmer or merchant along the eastern line of rail has a growing feeling of identification with the B.P. Some are apprehensive again, but also proud of the territory's accomplishments in economics and in maintaining racial tranquillity. A stock fence on the Republican side of the Transvaal-Tuli border has not only limited some movement in regard to grazing and water, but has been something of a psychological force as well.

English- and Afrikaans-speaking farmers in the Tuli block, seven miles wide and three hundred miles long, had a resurgence of feeling for South Africa in late 1963.

However, their late member on the Legislative Council,
L. van Gass, advised strongly against the proposal to set
up a pro-South Africa white political party. Such a step
would be political suicide for local whites within an overwhelmingly African country, and is unlikely to be viewed
favourably by the South African authorities themselves,
who have enough to do without struggling with Britain over
more rights for such farmers than any citizen in the B.P.
will be given.

The Tati Concession, occupying the northeast part of the
Protectorate, dates from a grant by the Matabele chief
Lobengula on 2 September 1880. It has always had close
ties with Southern Rhodesia. Indeed, the Southern Rhodesian Government made official representations in the
1930s, when South Africa was pressing for incorporation, to
protect its legal position in the event of Bechuanaland being
dismembered. The Tati Company owns most of Francistown and tremendous blocks of farming land. In 1955,
control of the company passed from London to Johannesburg, where the Glazer Brothers' financial combine has its
headquarters. At first, the new owners began insisting on
legal, but largely lapsed, rights, and generally 'turned on
the screws'. More recently, and largely as a result of
Bechuanaland Government pressure, they have begun to
ameliorate a few of the anachronistic arrangements. Some of
these involve the collection of taxes from African farmers,
and on township building sites. The arrears of taxes grow
in numerous categories, and the British Government would
be extremely reluctant to attempt to enforce collection. In
fact, it has caused special legislation to be passed to enable
the B.P. Government to take over the management of
water and light in Francistown from the Tati Company.

One curious sidelight: one house in Francistown is
occupied by refugees. A private British group, 'The Joint
Committee for the High Commission Territories', owns the
house, but the Tati Company owns the land. The Company
has refused rent and demands that the refugees be moved.

Since 1963, D. Mincher, a son-in-law of the late South African Prime Minister Field Marshal J. C. Smuts, has been put in local charge of the company properties in the B.P. He is personally affable and able; local residents are awaiting experience to determine whether he has significant authority to solve thorny local problems. While it is true that in South Africa the evocation of the famous Boer leader and world statesman, Smuts, is impressive to English-speaking whites, the political times are such in Bechuanaland that African leaders, particularly in the B.P.P., do not make sharp distinctions between the National Party and the United Party in South Africa. General Smuts' reputation in the crushing of the Bondelswart rebellion, whether his decisions are judged in a friendly or critical fashion, was not such as to inspire African enthusiasm. South African companies which may consider themselves 'liberal' in their local context often have difficulty adjusting to the present realities of modern Africa outside the Republic.

To return to the Tati, there has been intermittent agitation on the part of some Europeans that it should join with Southern Rhodesia. This has ebbed away as the Federation of Rhodesia and Nyasaland has collapsed, and the political tensions between black and white in Southern Rhodesia have grown over the last five years. Early in 1963, a delegation of European farmers called upon their local member of the legislature with an eye to secession, but he convinced them that they did not want to join any other country, but really were asking for independence—an impracticable goal. By August 1963, the writer could find very little sentiment for either independence or for association with Southern Rhodesia. But while the feeling of being a part of Bechuanaland has grown steadily in the Tati Concession, the fear of an African Government continues to alarm some interests there.

The opening of the new Mopani Club for all races startled some whites, although non-racial clubs seemed to an outsider not only natural but inevitable. A certain ostracism of the then District Commissioner, Phillip Steenkamp, a Kenya-born Afrikaner, by members of the 'white club' because of his championing of the African cause, led to some tension between Steenkamp and his colleagues in the Administration.

A meeting in Francistown was addressed by a Pretoria lawyer, Lourens Beyers, who argued that the British Government has made the 1·324 million acres a white territory by confirming the freehold ownership of concession land in 1911. One Tati farmer took the line in December 1963 that 'Fifty years ago we voluntarily accepted British protection; should Britain grant the Bechuanas independence, we can break away if we want to.'

All talk of secession of European parts of the B.P., either for the purpose of joining with another white-dominated state or to form a pocket-size country, has been scorned by Seretse Khama, and is adamantly opposed by virtually all the chiefs and leading Bechuanas.

In Bechuanaland as a whole there has been a remarkable surge of national consciousness since 1960. Further hesitation in European 'loyalty', and even foolish statements and minor actions by Europeans may be expected. That 'white' emotions towards the emerging nation are ambivalent is perhaps not surprising. But any serious moves would require the backing of a cautious South African Government, as we shall see. Among the vast African majority, there is no group, tribe, or region which now wants to secede. The potential desire of the Hereros in Ngamiland to the north and west for affiliation with South West Africa has not developed. Unhappy as they are with Batawana rule in Maun and elsewhere, their desire is to return to South West, from whence they fled German wrath two generations ago, but does not include the physical linking up of their present lands with those of their brothers in South West. Some Angolan Africans prefer to live in Ngamiland near the Caprivi Strip border, but there is very little contact across the Strip into Angola by Africans, private Europeans, or the British administration.

In the light of this psychological 'raising of the boundaries' of the territory, the location of the national capital at the Imperial Reserve (Mafeking) in the Cape Province of South Africa becomes more anomalous than ever.

Gaberones Capital

Her Majesty's Commissioner Peter Fawcus and the British Government attach great political significance to the building from scratch of a new Bechuanaland capital at Gaberones. The dam for an adequate water supply is under construction, and it is planned that the first transfers of departments should take place at the beginning of 1965.

While there is no legal discrimination in offices, family housing, sports, etc., in the Imperial Reserve at Mafeking, the general pattern of discrimination in the town itself cannot fail to have its effect upon the relationships of African and European members of the Administration. Although the South African Government has leaned over backwards to accommodate the Territorial headquarters, and the movement of officials of all races to and from the B.P. is without hindrance, the situation remains a drag on felicitous race relations. For one thing, Seretse Khama is a member of the Executive Council of the Legislature. One reason weekly Exco meetings, as well as the periodic sessions of Legco itself, are held in Lobatsi is because Seretse Khama who is a member was named a prohibited immigrant to South Africa at the time of his marriage. A second reason was a conscious desire on the part of Government to 'move into the Territory'.

The loss of the Protectorate headquarters will be a sharp economic blow to the town of Mafeking. In its edition of 30 June 1961 the Mafeking *Mail* proposed an exchange of land between Bechuanaland and South Africa. This was to create a corridor a few miles wide and sixteen miles long, to allow the headquarters site to become legally part of the B.P. In exchange, land of comparable value would be given to South Africa towards South West Africa, where the border is not well drawn from a strategic viewpoint. I interviewed various responsible officials, including the Mayor at that time, Mr. Frankel. (Mafeking is one of several predominantly Afrikaans towns which periodically have a Jewish Mayor.) While he personally would have liked to find a *modus vivendi* for retaining the B.P. administration, the Mayor said the proposal had not even been seriously put to the South African authorities.

The reason such an exchange was not favoured on the British side is that, even with a corridor, the location of the capital at the extreme southern tip of the Protectorate would perpetuate a sense of isolation between country and capital, and could not make a positive political contribution to a new national spirit.

As plans are now developing for Gaberones, all racial barriers, which existed not only in the environment of Mafeking but traditionally almost as strongly throughout the territory, would be wiped away. In a new environment, the chances of encouraging non-racial social patterns would be enhanced.

The need for this is evident when one studies the results of the recent legal desegregation in Bechuanaland. In Francistown hotels, for example, the European boycott of the better bars has faded away, but by one means or another the two racial groups have avoided each other in public places.

Because of the persistence of older racial patterns in most parts of the B.P., the establishment of the new capital at Gaberones on a non-racial basis, and fairly near the centre of most tribes and population, promises to be a powerful force in the new sense of Bechuanaland nationhood.

Constitutional Advance

In June 1964 Her Majesty's Government accepted in general the recommendations for constitutional change in

Bechuanaland put forward from the Territory (in Legislative Council Paper No. 9 of 1963/4: according to this document the recommendations were reached unanimously). The first step will be a general election in March 1965. The new Legislature will comprise an Upper and a Lower House. The latter will consist of approximately thirty-two members elected for a maximum of five years (the precise number of seats will depend on the delimitation of constituencies). There will also be four members chosen without regard to race by the elected members. The Prime Minister will nominate candidates for these seats but other legislators may add to the list of nominees. This provision may draw in specially qualified people who would not wish to stand in a constituency, or make it possible for special interests such as the business community or even a racial group such as the Asians to be represented. Since these seats can only be filled with the support of the elected members it is unlikely that contentious individuals will be elected to them.

Election will be by universal adult suffrage; the franchise does not mention race and applies to both sexes equally. Provision is made for those working away from Bechuanaland, but for the actual registration and voting an elector must return to his polling station. Provision is also made for a Bill of Rights similar to those included in the constitutions of Kenya and Uganda.

The Legislature will be elected by registered voters in single-member constituencies divided on an equal population basis, with consideration of community of interest, transport lines, tribal boundaries, and sparsity of population. To run for office, a candidate must be able to speak and read English well enough to participate in debates.

The Upper House of Chiefs will be composed of the eight tribal heads in the B.P. and four additional members elected by them. It will have advisory powers, particularly in regard to matters of traditional authority.

Under the new arrangements the present Executive Council will be replaced by a Cabinet made up of Her Majesty's Commissioner, a Prime Minister, a Deputy Prime Minister, up to five other ministers drawn from the Legislative Assembly and the Financial Secretary. The latter will be *ex officio* Minister of Finance. The Attorney General will normally attend Cabinet meetings in an advisory capacity, and will later be replaced by a Minister from the Legislature.

Her Majesty's Commissioner will retain control of external affairs and defence. He will also be responsible for the appointment and discipline of Public Service Officers on the advice of an independent Public Service Commission and, in association with the Prime Minister, for internal security. He will have power to dissolve the Legislature if the Prime Minister so requests and if a vote of no-confidence has been passed, or if the post of Prime Minister becomes vacant and there is no prospect of a candidate gaining majority support.

Thus Bechuanaland is about to take a long constitutional step forward. A clean break will be made not only with racialism and with members nominated by the representatives of the British Government, but also with tribalism in the highest government of the country.

No doubt, some thoughtful men are apprehensive over such a radical change at one fell swoop. It would seem, however, that any less advanced system would not have set the African leadership a sufficiently challenging task nor have lasted long enough to become truly workable. The Bechuanaland arrangements go beyond the new Transkei constitution principally in the virtual elimination of traditional rule in the central Government. Furthermore, they imply a more rapid advance to full independence than has been suggested for the Transkei. The comparison is highly significant because of the offer made by Prime Minister Verwoerd to present his case to the Bechuana

people on the question of their possible association with
South Africa.

An objective observer cannot fail to note that materially
greater improvements are being made in the Transkei than
in Bechuanaland. If Britain could turn the Protectorates
from the poor country cousins of southern Africa into
something of a shop window for vigorous non-racial
government, the changed situation would not be without an influence upon public thinking within the Republic
itself.

Experience gained in Ghana, Nigeria, Tanganyika,
Uganda, and Kenya was evident in the whole approach to,
and conduct of, the constitutional talks. Many earlier
pitfalls have been avoided. That is not to say that sweet-
ness and light will necessarily be the chief qualities of the
life of the constitution when it comes into effect. But the
problems will be new ones rather than those Britain learned
from further north in Africa. The bargaining behind
the scenes this time was never full of such suspicion,
paternalism, and even bitterness as characterised earlier
conferences of this nature in Africa. The pledges to African
peoples which Britain has redeemed in the last decade
have won her respect from those over whom the Union
Jack still flies.

No two colonial constitutions are the same but the
Bechuanaland one coming into effect is unusual in that it
transfers control from an official to an unofficial legislature
while retaining a large share of the power in official hands.
This is only possible because of the unanimous support for
the constitutional changes by the existing members of
Legco and also a general feeling of trust and confidence
between the British Administration and the peoples of the
territory. Without such a feeling the Legislature and Her
Majesty's Commissioner would be at constant loggerheads
and a series of constitutional crises would result. Although
not without calculated risks, the new constitution is a

brilliant example of a particular adaptation to a particular time and situation. Furthermore, it is based upon the assumption that even these new changes are but an interim step towards full independence.

III. ECONOMIC DEVELOPMENT

The B.P., in common with many developing countries, has a one-product economy. Not only are 87 per cent of exports based upon livestock, but improvements in national income have tended to increase the relative importance of cattle.

Such dependence is highly risky. Drought is a recurring visitor to this low-rainfall country. Disease could sweep the herds as foot and mouth disease has in South West Africa. For Bechuanaland, control would be more difficult and the consequences more catastrophic. Competition in African markets and overseas is a constant threat to the national income from economic forces alone, not to mention political pressures.

And yet developing countries do not often have the alternatives that might theoretically be attractive. In some new African countries, so much attention has been focused upon avoiding economic exploitation and in choosing who may invest that all investors have tended to stay away and make controls purely academic. In cold reality, Bechuanaland is compelled to play from its strength. The best middle term prospects for greater national income lie in quantitative gains in livestock production, further local processing to add value to the product, expansion of markets by volume, and the obtaining of higher prices. At present, some 98 per cent of the people within the country are dependent upon cattle for subsistence and cash income. It may well be possible to reduce this concentration of employment without reducing the national income from livestock.

Cash savings in the B.P. are minimal and the transition from a barter economy based upon cattle is far from complete. If Britain has in the past kept Bechuanaland from being swallowed up, its contribution to education and its aid to capital formation have not been impressive. The

background assumption of eventual political transfer to
South Africa had kept British development contributions
unusually low even a decade after World War II. Private
investment has likewise been inhibited by political uncertainty, just as similar fears played a part in the slow development of such other African countries as Tanganyika and
Togoland.

Only indigenous African leadership can call for and
demand the kinds of economic sacrifice which sometimes
succeed in helping capital formation in poor countries. The
imposition of greater economic stringency by a British
Government would not have been politically feasible in
the B.P., any more than Her Majesty's Government could
introduce the compulsory cutting out of diseased cocoa trees
in the best interests of the people of Ghana, a step an
African Government could and did take.

Viewed in the present-day world, Bechuanaland has a
chance to profit from another side of the colonial relationship; namely, the generous treatment Great Britain has
given to some newly independent African states now within
the Commonwealth. The United Kingdom is the B.P.'s
great and sure source of financial sympathy and capital
support.

African rule in Bechuanaland could mean greater local
savings. Many of these might be less in cash than in contributions of voluntary labour released in the emotional
dam-burst of independence. However, the popular and
pressing and understandable cry for education and services
may drown appeals for saving. Capital for investment is
more likely to come from direct access to international
agencies and foreign Governments on the one hand, and
from private investors on the other, when the latter are
convinced that the new African leadership can maintain
stable government.

A second unusual advantage of Bechuanaland is its
physical proximity to South Africa, and especially to the
booming Witwatersrand. Few undeveloped countries are

as accessible to highly developed countries as Bechuanaland; the relationship of Puerto Rico to the United States has points in parallel. A short distance away, inside the same financial system and customs wall, lie great monetary institutions, advanced educational facilities, and enormously complex and diversified skills. Bechuanaland does need its first dentist, but not a wide range of dental specialists. It is hard to realise the savings in money, time, and general efficiency of having nearby specialists and research stations.

And yet, as we will see, the political factors involved in the proximity of South Africa balance and may outweigh the economic advantages.

Migrant Labour

The fact that thousands of Bechuanas work in the Republic is itself very much a mixed blessing. At all times 20 per cent of the adult male population are away working in South Africa, the motivation being primarily the lack of employment in Bechuanaland. A prestige factor has also developed since labour migration started about 1870, attaching to the man who has been to the 'big city', possibly undertaken dangerous mine work, and who returns home with presents and savings (translated into head of cattle) for his family.

When remittances, savings, and goods are added up, migrant workers bring into the territory about £1.3 million annually.

On one hand, the territory loses the most productive years of the ablest members of the society, but on the other, some of the skills acquired in the city are transmitted to tribal life. However, most Bechuana work as mine labourers and acquire few skills, whereas the Basuto, for example, tend to secure the better jobs in and out of the mines. A significant by-product of migration is that the westernised sojourners tend to lose their respect for tribal authority. Now for those migrants outside the mines, this may be

replaced by some sophistication in western political organisation. This is rarely true of those in the mines where the
non-Bechuana associates are likely to be migrant workers
from another extra-South African territory. Thus, they
may lose respect for traditional authority without gaining
understanding or respect for a new authority beyond the
routine of compound living and African 'boss boys'.

The great student of Bechuana migration, Professor I.
Schapera, has also stressed that migration leads to indis-
cipline among women and children. Although the mine
migrants were originally responsible for introducing tuberculosis, syphilis, and other diseases into Bechuanaland,
they are no longer alone in this regard. Schapera has found
that migration leads to a later marriage age, and that this
has encouraged promiscuity. He suggests that the birth
rate is negatively affected in several ways by migration.

One of the easiest armchair recommendations to stop
migration evils is to suggest that migration be stopped.
Political leaders in West Africa have also pointed out the
political desirability of ceasing to send Bechuanas into
'apartheid country'. This cannot be because of a belief
that migratory labour, *per se*, is evil, even where it is acknowledged to be undesirable. Thousands of Africans from
neighbouring French-speaking territories migrate season-
ally to the cocoa belt of Ashanti for work on the land.
Similarly, across the continent in Uganda, the migration
for one or two years of Banyaruanda to work in the Baganda-
owned cotton fields of Buganda, while down from an annual
peak of 100,000 plus, is still an immensely important labour
migration. The difference for Bechuana migrants is that
they go to work for 'white' masters, not black ones, even
though they may receive higher pay and more material
benefits.

However, Schapera's reasons why, in 1947, he would not
recommend statutory attempts to restrict migrants, still have
much of their force today. In the long run, it is the social
and economic development of the B.P. which must provide

local employment and so fill the need which led poor and hungry migrants to the Witwatersrand in the first place. Progress is being made, for there are hundreds of Bechuanas gainfully at work in the territory today who, a generation ago, would have found their only employment opportunity in South Africa. The B.P. Department of Education has searched in South Africa by advertisement and by personal contacts for expatriate Bechuana degree holders and others potentially able to assume educational posts in their own country. Unfortunately, as we have noted, Bechuanas have not acquired skills so frequently as other African expatriates in the Republic.

Thus, the pragmatic case for slowing down and eventually ending migratory labour is economically convincing, and will be brought about through economic growth in the B.P. itself, all of which leads us to consider the broad educational picture.

Education and Manpower

Although maximum effort has been directed to education through decades of lean budgets, and generations of devoted officials and teachers, both African and European, have done their best, the educational standards of the B.P. are miserably low. Raising them is the prime development task. Where to concentrate limited educational resources is a difficult question, which will be considered after a brief review of the territory's educational development.

Missionaries, and particularly the London Missionary Society, took the lead in establishing the early schools. One of the first was in the present Bakwena Reserve where David Livingstone had lived about 1845. A tribal pattern of schooling has persisted into the era of primarily govern-mental financing. Although the Tribal School Committees run the schools, the syllabuses, etc., are under the control of the Government Education Department.

As the Government has pointed out, tribal management 'ensures a very large degree of genuine local interest in education and affords invaluable opportunities for training in committee work and in financial management'. What is recognised, but not often said, is that it also allows for financial mismanagement, a loss in planning efficiency when the tribes are taken individually, and not the B.P. collectively, and also the problem so characteristic of American education, that poor areas have poor schools and rich states or tribes pull farther ahead. Out of some 218 primary schools, the Government directly administers 25, the missions only 9, and all but one other are run by Tribal School Committees. The curricula in all the schools follow the pattern and general content of British education, with some adaptations (history, biology) to Africa and the B.P.

About two-thirds of primary school pupils are girls. This reflects the use of young boys as cattle herders, and is in contrast with some agricultural parts of Africa where schools are flooded with boys, but the girls are kept back to help their mothers in the fields. Although there is still force in Aggrey's famous aphorism that to educate boys is to educate individuals, but to educate girls is to educate the family, and thus the nation, he applied it to environments where male education was ahead. In view of the present role of women in Bechuana society, it is doubtful whether the economic return on girls' education is now equal to that of boys.

Whereas primary school pupils are of the order of 50,000, secondary school totals have climbed steeply in recent years, but are still only just breaking the 1,000 level. About 60 per cent of these advanced students are boys. Moeng College (secondary) in Bamangwato territory enrolled more girls than boys among its 250 pupils for the first term in 1962. It is doubtful whether fifty primary students to one secondary student is a wise ratio.

Probably the greatest financial wastage in Bechuanaland has occurred in education. When a boy leaves a cattle post for three or four years of schooling, he will not really become usefully literate. No studies have been made of 'lost literacy' in Bechuanaland, but the existence of the problem is not doubted. In many cases, he returns to the cattle and never reads a book again in his life. The lack of useful application of knowledge on the part of girls who drop out in primary years is as great.

General education is good like motherhood, Santa Claus, and piety. But educational monies are as scarce in the B.P. as water. They must not be sprinkled indiscriminately across the educational desert where illiteracy may be 80 per cent, but should be carefully husbanded to be used where maximum human returns are possible, to the end that education for all will come in as few decades as possible.

The able Director of Education, Mr. Jack Hunter, and his staff, including Miss Chiepe, the leading African educationalist, are aware of the present situation. The hard choice is between providing school for all or placing a greater emphasis on primary school completions and, above all, on the secondary school level. It appears politically impossible to cut back on primary schools, and even cruel to deny struggling centres more schools. But it is likely that the greatest economic returns will come from emphasising quality over quantity. Whether African leaders in power will be able to resist local demands is doubtful. Eastern Nigeria, for example, as a result of political pressure, probably spends too much money on primary schools to the detriment of creating jobs for those who finish them.

It is a common phenomenon of developing countries, first noticed so sharply in India, that a surplus of partially educated people mushrooms. This is already noticeable at the lower clerk level in B.P. In the early 1950s in Ghana, there were positions for any young man who had completed some secondary schooling. But by 1960, I became increasingly conscious of the large numbers of unemployed and casually employed school-leavers hanging around street corners. On the one hand, they felt themselves too educated for agriculture and disliked tribal authority, but on the other hand, they were not well enough educated to find white-collar employment. As they grew in numbers, they constituted a potentially explosive political pressure group. It was in part to meet this threat that Dr. Kwame Nkrumah created the Builders Brigades modelled on the American depression-spawned C.C.C. (Civilian Conservation Corps). It is possible to return detribalised youths to the country-side for roadbuilding, dam making, and harvesting, if they are organised and inspired along modern city lines.

Although Bechuanaland already does have unemployed clerk types, there were never greater opportunities for the able young Bechuana. The present school-going generation has a limitless political, economic, and social future. Mobility of all kinds will never be higher in the history of the gestating nation.

Bechuanaland resembles most developing African countries in that the educational bottleneck is the secondary school. But it is different in lacking the university opportunities so relatively abundant in Africa. Once through secondary school, it is easier for an African to get into a good university in Africa than for an American to get into a good institution in his country. The present unused capacity of most African universities will be filled as new secondary schools contribute their streams, but today able Bechuanas could find admittance in many parts of the continent.

It may be said in jest, but also with truth, that what the steel mill is as a symbol to developing Asian countries, the university is to developing African countries. African leaders and British officials in the B.P. all agree today that a university is beyond the foreseeable financial capability of the territory. The number of Bechuanas currently studying at universities is only twenty. Sharp percentage increases are likely, but an output of hundreds of advanced students is at least a decade ahead. Meanwhile, the question is, where will Bechuanas go who do carry on their education? In the past, the majority of them have obtained various forms of higher education in South Africa. The Tiger Kloof Mission institution in the Republic educated a substantial number of Bechuana leaders. At a higher academic level, Fort Hare played a role before it became an ethnic institution for Xhosa speakers. But for a variety of reasons, South Africa is unlikely to be the site of much Bechuana degree work.

Official arrangements currently provide for Bechuanas to attend the secular University College in Basutoland, which grew out of the Pius XII College near Maseru. There is a favourable linguistic background in that both territories are Sotho-speaking, but in any event, the instruction would be in English. It is likely that as new institutions develop nearer by, such as the Zambia University, Bechuana students will never be thus concentrated in Basutoland. In this part of Africa, the political flux makes long-range assumptions for higher education uncertain. This is not serious for Bechuanaland, where small numbers make it unnecessary to blueprint precisely where and how higher education will be organised.

The economic development of the B.P. is intertwined with its political growth; the stability of the latter is a prerequisite for success in the former. What is needed on both fronts is a substantial flow of men and women who have completed a good post-primary education. In Africa today, as in Britain or the U.S. a generation ago, a man needs a secondary education as a launching pad from which his own abilities will have a chance to take over.

In comparative educational terms, Bechuanaland is un-like Ghana, where the writer estimated in 1950 that there were about 1,200 living graduates. It is like the Congo, where the number of graduates, not including African priests, was of the order of sixteen at the time of independence. The Congo is a tremendous territory, and the anarchy following independence was disastrous in the lives of average Congolese. I was an observer in the Congo in

1960 during the worst of the fighting and raping. But those who would hold up the Congo as an example of African inability to rule, or would emphasise the limited number of graduates, must also take note of the recently demonstrated abilities of some hundreds of Congolese leaders whose formal education ended with secondary school. Bechuanaland's population is not much larger than that of greater Leopoldville; it lacks the tribal antipathies; and its economic problems are of a far lower order than those of the Congo. Given the sound foundation of a substantial outflow of good secondary-school-educated men, Bechuanaland will be a well-run African country. It is the priceless advantage permeating the whole educational life of the B.P. to be moving towards independence without the political bitterness of the Congo, with far more trust between white and black, and a present Administration whose success will be measured by how successful a self-governing Bechuanaland will be, and not how long this stage is delayed.

Since 1 January 1964, all State-aided schools in Bechuanaland have been open to qualified students regardless of race. That is to say that European children are free to enter Sechuana-medium schools if they have sufficient command of the tongue, and Bechuana children with adequate English cannot be refused admission to English-medium schools. The linguistic distinction could be, but is not, a device for racial segregation.

A particularly thorny problem closely related to education is the recruitment of skilled manpower. To be sure, Bechuanaland has a capable civil service of Europeans and Africans, and Africanisation if gradual should be possible without loss of efficiency. But again, politics are important, specifically in the attitude of the African leaders and the British Government to the employment of South Africans. Approximately half the civil servants, and many of those acknowledged the most capable, are South African-born.

But many have devoted their careers to work in the Protectorate and identify themselves closely with its people and its problems.

However, the British Government, acting on advice from a visiting expert, and not necessarily with the concurrence of local British-born officials, has seen fit to discriminate against Bechuanaland civil servants on the grounds of their place of original employment, and to all intents and purposes on nationality rather than on merit. It has been said that an extraordinarily able Director of Agriculture was lost to the territory as a result of such a discriminatory approach. A completely convincing case could be made against anyone born in South Africa, or anywhere else, whose attitude and actions towards Africans smacked of racial prejudice. But the official referred to was so highly regarded as a person, Afrikaner or not, that groups of Bechuana farmers went out of their way to honour him with parties on his departure. Good grounds can be found for suddenly clearing the security police of South Africans by transferring them to less sensitive work, although some of them were not happy that twenty years of unblemished service counted for nothing against the new criterion of which country they came from. But there is a feeling in the Bechuanaland civil service that there are now two classes of civil servants, and what counts most for retirement and, to a lesser extent, for promotion, in the eyes of London, is birthplace and not ability. This is not to say that no South Africans are promoted.

Her Majesty's Commissioner has stressed to the writer that the overseas aid scheme is intended to provide special inducements to members of Her Majesty's Overseas Civil Service and certain other officers recruited by the Secretary of State, mainly in administrative or professional posts, for which there is a shortage of applicants. Most of these officers are from the United Kingdom, but some of the senior South African officers are also designated under the scheme. No South Africans have been required to retire.

The Bechuanaland Government is taking the future employment of South Africans under consideration, because it is felt officially that the employment of aliens is not normal. In addition to the process of Africanisation, the B.P. Government is taking special care with new 'European' appointments. Officers of any race who are recruited in southern Africa do not share in the expatriate and inducement elements of the overseas officers.

All of this is the source of a good deal of heartburning in the service and it remains in most African countries a ticklish problem to which independence has brought no easy solution. For the first years after Ghanaian independence, the Professor of Agriculture at the University College and a majority of his staff were white South African citizens. In Bechuanaland, it would not be easy to replace the many able men in non-political positions such as livestock inspectors. One might expect that the test should be whether they will serve well and with respect under an Africanised Government, and not whether under the British lead they will be forced out of their positions. The transition in Ghana and in Nigeria and Uganda was smoothly and efficiently handled for the most part. But white South Africans are treated equally with white people generally. The present discrimination in many independent African countries such as Tanganyika against even the most liberal white journalist or minister of religion from the Republic is however an indication of possible future trouble. Bechuanaland is not the first country in which the special South African issue has arisen. Virtually all the British-employed South Africans in Basutoland have been discharged or transferred elsewhere in response to Basuto pressures. When and if a similar pattern unfolds in Bechuanaland, some large-scale manpower adjustments will have to be made.

Despite whatever arrangements may be made to retain efficient and loyal South African-born civil servants, as well as those provided from the United Kingdom, one can expect a higher than normal rate of attrition as independence approaches. What are the prospects for replacement beyond the education of Bechuanas we have described? Egypt is about the only country to the north with a surplus of educated personnel. Black Africa needs the people it now has and will not have an 'export' of men for some years. Probably the best source of skilled Africans is the Republic of South Africa, where the educational system— in purely academic terms—was long in advance of any country south of the Sahara. Educated Africans, among them 49,000 with professional qualifications, are not utilised to their maximum effectiveness, nor paid so well as whites with the same degrees, and many may willingly work in a neighbouring country to escape onerous restrictions in their personal lives. Indeed, the danger that Sesuto-speaking Africans from the Republic may 'move in' on Bechuanaland posts is not without its dangers of friction. In Maun, the capital of Ngamiland, one hears whispers against the ruling Regent because she is a South African-born girl from the Orange Free State, although she has been in Maun for twenty years and other Bechuana chiefs have married South African girls.

Tribal and national prejudice are likewise barriers to imports from other parts of Africa. Ghana did not have an altogether successful experience with imported West Indians in such fields as the judiciary. Americans of African descent have many psychological problems stemming from their resentment if they are not accepted as Africans and the contrary resentment if they are accepted. The level of salaries Bechuanaland can pay is a limiting factor. It is likely that individuals—not excluding all Europeans—from throughout Africa and elsewhere will find acceptance and make a contribution on an individual basis. But no outside group would seem to be 'the answer' to Bechuanaland's short-term and middle-term skilled manpower problems. Some help may come from the many capable Bechuana who live in the western Transvaal and, although often limited in formal education, hold what are practically speaking skilled positions in the industrial complex of the Republic.

Cattle Industry

Cattle are the lifeblood of the B.P., the principal form of savings, basis of the major export industry, and the greatest asset for immediate increases in national income. Although cattle are also the esteemed form of wealth and have great cultural significance, the Bechuana will and do sell their beasts. The 'Masai problem' of large herds without practical economic value, over-grazing, erosion, and more over-grazing, is not so thorny as it has been in East Africa. The Bechuana cattle sales handle a reasonable annual offtake of 6 per cent. In 1963, exports were 130,000— about 10 per cent. This could be raised, experts feel, to even 15 per cent.

Africans own about 90 per cent of the cattle, and the tendency among most owners, with notable exceptions among African owners of larger herds and Europeans, is to place quantity above quality. Cattle are owned by the head of the family in trust. The Bechuana are careful about slaughtering cattle for their own consumption, and a change in eating patterns does not now threaten to reduce the numbers available for export. Cattle are at present essential for ploughing, hauling wagons, and as a source of dairy products.

African-owned cattle are normally herded in the bare, unfenced veld. Herds are kept at 'cattle posts' under the care of employees, and often great distances from the main towns where the Bechuana owners may live. The posts are sited with reference to available grass, the flat pans of water which persist long after rains, and the water points drilled by the Government, tribal authorities, or private syndicates. Some good grazing land is not utilised because of drought. The territory's average carrying capacity is low at one beast per fifty acres.

The Bamangwato, Barolong, and Bakgatla tribes maintain their own livestock improvement centres. The directions of improvement which involve no technical problem, but rather wider education and social acceptance, include introduction of better bulls on a systematic basis and not the occasional effort now made; selling cattle at a younger age and not using up valuable grazing on aged beasts; culling out the unfit animals and castrating the inferior bulls. Strenuous efforts have been made to protect grazing, especially in the vicinity of watering points where grass is under the heaviest pressure. Greater control is necessary in the interests of all cattle owners. The Bakgatla, under a strong chief, have set an excellent pattern in controlling grazing with a general limit of 500 head near a borehole; many of their boreholes are developed by syndicates of cattle owners.

It is unlikely that a Government of Africans would be able to issue stronger orders than some chiefs do now. However, in the B.P. as a whole, an African Government could enforce stricter regulations with stiffer penalties and probably be more persuasive as well in enlisting the co-operation of cattle owners. On the other hand, the political pressures on vulnerable African politicians might well be so great that worse misuse of natural resources could result. The sharp increase in poaching and lack of effective control in some newly-independent African states shows this other side of the coin.

An African Government will undoubtedly wish to reduce its dependence upon South Africa for a wide range of veterinary assistance. South African research and provision of vaccines have been a major factor in improving B.P. cattle. It will cost money to replace what South Africa has willingly supplied in kind through the years. This is not to mention that the great majority of veterinarians and cattle inspectors in the B.P. have been recruited in the Republic with greater experience and lower costs than would be involved in bringing such men from elsewhere. A negative side of this may have been to postpone the training of Bechuana technicians and inspectors for the cattle industry. But the abrupt termination of scientific and personnel relationships with South Africa would seriously cripple the expansion of the cattle industry.

The great strides in the industry have been made in marketing. Just a decade ago, all cattle were marketed on the hoof. Today, the Lobatsi Abattoir, started by the Colonial Development Corporation, processes up to 90 per cent of the cattle exported. The value of such cattle has been running at an annual rate of £2.1 million. The C.D.C. venture is an outstanding example of successful development, not only in its economic achievements, but in winning the acceptance of the indigenous population. The total C.D.C. investment in Bechuanaland is £1,859,000, compared with £19,488,000 in Swaziland and £200,000 in Basutoland.

In an effort to give the abattoir more 'grass roots' in the B.P., the Government has already secured shares in the enterprise, as have a group of trustees acting on behalf of the producers. Profits in excess of 6 per cent are devoted to various schemes to assist cattle production in the territory. It is not unlikely that in the long run the ownership of the abattoir will be in the hands of Bechuanas and thus conclude a bright chapter in the colonial development book. This is not to ignore many current and potential problems. Demands for a second abattoir in Francistown have been persistent and not without long-range sense. However, the premature launching of a second venture could financially jeopardise both abattoirs.

Markets in Africa are subject to the usual price vicissitudes and to political changes. In the long run, the Congo and Angola markets are full of promise. Ngamiland at present sells much of its cattle to the Rhodesias because of great distance from the railroad and from Lobatsi. Lacking a seaport, the B.P. is dependent upon its neighbours for access to world markets. The present route for chilled carcasses through Mafeking, south to Cape Town, and eventually onto the British table, is obviously dependent upon a stable and unhostile South Africa. A boycott of South African ports by Bechuanaland meat exports would have even less impact than similar action by Northern Rhodesia and Nyasaland against Angolan and Mozambique ports, respectively. At present, these African countries would be cutting their throats in order to inflict minor wounds on a potential adversary. Bechuanaland could refuse to sell meat in the South African market to the delight of South and South West African producers. The cold facts are that the strategic geography of southern Africa strongly favours South Africa and the Portuguese territories.

The long-range prospects for B.P. cattle are excellent. No major breakthrough in technology is required. The great potential boon is discovery and use of additional water resources. But even without such good fortune or Okavango development, the steady (if limited) investment of capital, and the continued education efforts of Government departments, promise an even greater contribution to the gross national product. It is politically significant that this resource, so vital to the B.P., is intimately bound up in the life of its people. Although technical change may be slowed up by the need to educate illiterate people and to change established customs, Bechuanaland does not resemble some Middle Eastern oil countries in which the most advanced technology imported by aliens never becomes an integral part of the lives of the people, failing to benefit them in non-material ways, with the result that such a dichotomy occurs in the national life that political stability is threatened. Even if attractive alternatives are presented to the development of the cattle industry, political common sense would dictate that the role of the cattle industry at least keep pace with mineral or industrial development.

Agriculture

Crops are the poor cousin of cattle in both financial importance and status. And yet the B.P. faces an immediate need for greater agricultural production if profits from selling meat are not to be consumed in importing food for a growing population.

The 1960 economic survey mission estimated the total arable land of the B.P. at 8 million acres, of which about 5 per cent was under cultivation. African dryland farms are estimated to produce crops valued at some £1,000,000, primarily for local consumption. Expansion is possible for sorghum, millet, and groundnuts. Maize or American corn is a dubious crop under low and unreliable rainfall.

Poor agricultural practices characterise the territory. Animal manure is not applied to the fields, seeding is haphazard, and field cleanliness ignored. Maize is the principal crop, followed by sorghum (kaffir corn), which is more resistant to drought. Threshing is done by beating with long sticks. The handful of European farmers show maize yields from ten to fifteen times those of African farmers, an indication of what better techniques would mean to the bulk of the Bechuana farmers.

The practice of farmers living in villages far from the communal fields and not fencing them, when added to the primitive methods of ploughing, explains in part why only 5 per cent of the potential arable land (given present water supplies) is under cultivation. A final indication of the low level of agriculture is the need to import maize from South Africa and, indirectly, to export labour to South Africa.

The Bechuana have always lived in big towns by African standards. The town is divided into wards in which closely related people live together. Each ward has its own *kgotla* or meeting place. The traditional houses are strongly and neatly built, and these are not temporary settlements such as are found in most of the traditional Africa. This social organisation has meant close and efficient administration, and makes it possible to provide amenities for many people. On the other hand, we have mentioned the disadvantages of fields and cattle posts far from the towns. An adult Bechuana may do a considerable amount of travelling.

Characteristically for undeveloped countries, the most difficult and precarious farming—that most in need of technical knowledge and capital—is undertaken by those farmers who are least educated and most short of capital. Improvements in dryland African farming will be an uphill struggle under the best of circumstances, with Government relief efforts after droughts becoming a standard practice. Progressive African farmers complain that communal ownership of land discourages improvements, and that they cannot fence to improve their livestock. Fragmentation of land into smaller pieces and its location far from villages are further impediments to agricultural efficiency in the B.P., just as they are in other parts of the world, such as Bavaria. The custom persists in some parts that no African can plough his land until his own chief has given the signal and is another irritant to the farmer who may not have the same crops as most of his neighbours, or simply has other ideas on when to plant and when to harvest. This custom no doubt had validity in older tribal days when the chief and his advisers had a monopoly on accumulated knowledge of the seasons. Although anachronistic, it persists as a deterrent to better individual farming.

The most promising area for Government action is in the provision of improved storage facilities and in enhancing marketing facilities. Roads have made a noticeable difference in agricultural marketing in most of the Protectorate, and famine is no longer a threat in a small community.

The most promising means towards immediate and substantial production of cash crops, already pioneered by European farmers along the eastern strip, lies in irrigation. There are suitably fertile soils to repay the addition of fertilisers; and water and unexploited sources of water exist.

High yields are obtainable under the excellent conditions of summer. Winter frost, in part the result of rapid radiation on cloudless nights, limits the scope of tropical crops. One of the best recommended new crops is cotton, but it would require new marketing arrangements. The established groundnuts, maize and wheat (of which there is a shortage in South Africa) have already proved successful.

Again, politics intrude upon the economic scene. It is not politically feasible for the Government to spend large sums to help European farmers produce greater export crops, although it may be expected that African leaders will be careful not to lose what has been achieved. Expansion of irrigated farming will have a firm political footing if advanced African farmers are encouraged and assisted to play a substantial role. There are no racial restrictions upon African ownership of farms throughout the B.P., and a handful of Africans do farm in what are predominantly European farming areas. The Bamalete and Bangwaketse Reserves both have irrigation projects. New financial institutions to assist able Africans to farm on a larger than traditional scale may be required. All of this presumes that traditional tribal practices are incompatible with the high returns required from irrigated agriculture. Arrangements for some tribal units to enter such farming on a co-operative basis would be politically wise if administratively difficult.

Another avenue for improved income lies in expanding the dairy industry. The European farmers in the remote Ghanzi district have built up a fair-sized business by the sale of cream through South West Africa, and both Africans and Europeans produce for the Francistown creamery. Dairy income is running at a level of £145,000 annually. The industry is heavily dependent upon markets in neighbouring countries. A responsible Bechuana politician was approached with a request for him to advocate Bechuanaland's refusal to sell cream to certain countries as a political gesture. In reply, he said he would support such a move if those countries urging the step would buy Bechuanaland's cream for at least 75 per cent of the price now received. The offer was not accepted.

It is true of agriculture, as it is of almost every aspect of the economic life of the territory, that present scientific knowledge barely scratches the surface of its soil. Only the most general and isolated efforts have been made to study the soils of the whole territory, to experiment with possible crops, and to discover how present crop yields could be enhanced. A handful of devoted men have been struggling with problems that require more men and financing than has been available. For example, little work has been done on the commercial exploitation of timber in the few northern parts of the territory where rainfall is adequate.

Minerals

Bechuanaland is surrounded by some of the richest mining areas on the face of the globe. Not only does South Africa dominate world gold production, but it has a treasurehouse of other ores. South West Africa leads the world in producing gem diamonds and has a variety of metallic assets. Northern Rhodesia shares ownership of the copperbelt, with a quarter of the world's supply of copper. Southern Rhodesia has a profitable assortment of mines. Angola, a neighbour beyond the Caprivi Strip, has diamonds and oil.

The B.P. has very few mining areas. Asbestos and manganese are being mined on a modest scale in Bangwaketse land. B.P. manganese production in 1960 was 22,350 long tons. A new mine operates in Bamalete territory, in the south-eastern corner of the B.P. Here a Transvaal company aims at a monthly production of 5,000 tons. Minor gold and silver production in the Tati Concession has petered out. After three years of investigation, the Rhodesia Selection Trust (R.S.T.) is expected to decide shortly on plans to produce soda ash and sodium sulphate from the Makarikari Flats. Copper, lead and nickel are under investigation in Bamangwato tribal territory. Since 1959,

R.S.T. has had rights to 40,000 square miles and, in 1963, announced the finding of a copper mineralisation 60 miles west of Francistown. Low-grade coal fields have been proved on a large scale near the railroad north of Palapye and at Mamabula. Prospects for their commercial exploitation are at present not bright. Thus there is no bonanza on the scale of B.P.'s neighbours.

Is this a true reflection of the distribution of mineral resources? Simple logic would suggest that the lack of mineral discoveries in Bechuanaland is due in part to a lack of chance discovery in its vast and almost uninhabited parts. But to recall our geological description; in much of the territory the granite rocks are overlain by Kalahari sands and also by thin Karoo sedimentary rocks, so that discovery of underlying ores is not easy. The overburden would not be a major barrier to exploiting valuable discoveries. Successive refinements in methods of aerial prospecting offer real hope for making significant finds at economic costs. Results of a recent aerial survey which used advanced equipment for detecting the presence of magnetic ore bodies have not been publicly released.

Unpublished work by South African geologists in South West Africa suggests that a payable copper strike north and east of Windhoek may extend into, if not through, Bechuanaland, and even link up with the Northern Rhodesian copperbelt. There are other mineral-bearing formations in the Republic which dip under the surface in Bechuanaland.

Geological research is one more B.P. Government department where limited funds and a small staff have been inadquate to the immense task of achieving a detailed knowledge of the country and its resources. Given African control, it may be possible to induce outside investment groups to risk large sums on searching for payable minerals. Her Majesty's Government has been extraordinarily careful in the B.P., as it has usually been elsewhere, not to alienate local resources. Enough political repercussions have occurred in Africa to reveal how dangerous alienation can be. However, while new Governments are rightly cautious and sometimes over-suspicious of foreign investment, they can often afford greater political risks than the colonial power would take. A foreign investor can at least know that he will not be swept away in the anti-colonial tide.

To put a frank finger directly upon Bechuanaland's position, the most likely sources of enthusiasm, capital, and technical expertise are South Africa, and, secondly, Southern Rhodesia. But concessions in these quarters have long carried a particularly high political risk for Great Britain, and new ones to South African concerns now seem unlikely. It is quite in order for Ghana to buy gold mining machinery from South Africa; permissible for Ghana, Tanganyika, and the Soviet Union to market their diamonds through De Beers, and for various other independent African and Asian States to trade directly or *sub rosa* with South Africa. But a great storm would arise all the way from Legislative Council in Lobatsi to the General Assembly in New York if the U.K. were to sign a major concession arrangement with South African interests. An African Government, acting strictly according to what it felt were the best interests of the people of the territory, would be far freer to make concessions or to accept investment from groups in Johannesburg or Moscow. From the viewpoint of an African Government, great merit lies in the encouragement of investment from a variety of nations, including those not directly in the Cold War, as both Emperor Haile Selassie and President Tubman of Liberia have done so shrewdly.

At present, the mineral rights of the B.P. are widely and anachronistically dispersed. In tribal areas (including what is known as the Barolong farms), the tribe has the power to make or refuse concessions. Individuals who have sat through endless *kgotlas* (New England-type town meetings), trying to explain various provisions of agreements, are not enamoured of the system. The great danger for the B.P. as a whole is that a major discovery in one tribal area would lead to large revenues and presumably better roads and

schools, and a healthy standard of living for one tribe, while
a poor tribe would continue to suffer from financial mal-
nutrition.

The British South Africa Company (B.S.A. Co.) has the
mineral rights in the Lobatsi, Gaberones, and Tuli blocks,
as does the Tati Company in its concession. The B.S.A.
Company had similar rights in Northern Rhodesia, and
did not gain a reputation there for being a progressive
company with a deep interest in the welfare and the wishes
of the African inhabitants. In Northern Rhodesia, public
criticism of the B.S.A. Company was contrasted with
occasional praise for the activities of the Anglo American
and Rhodesian Selection Trust mining companies. As we
have seen, the Tati Company has had a poor image in
Bechuanaland. The political temperature in Bechuanaland
is such that antagonism between the concession holders
and the people of the territory is more likely to increase than
decrease. Investors may therefore hesitate to conclude
agreements with the holders of mineral rights. One may
anticipate a revision or even a buying back of some of the
present mineral rights held by outside interests.

The remainder of mineral rights cover Crown land and
are held by the British Government on behalf of the
Bechuana people. The only public prospecting allowed has
been in a small area opened to diamond prospectors since
1941. An overhaul and rationalisation of the system of
mineral concessions, so that greater control for the whole
B.P. lies in the hands of the central Government, appears
desirable to encourage mineral investigation, and to see
that any royalties are distributed in such a way as to maxi-
mise economic development.

Tourism

Probably no area of the B.P. economy could be more
immediately responsive to results than tourism. The Government is aware of this and is trying to encourage it. Its
potential has hardly been tapped. Bechuanaland has never

been a mecca for tourists. It lacks an international airport which so often prompts the flying tourist to stop off for a few days and it has no good tourist hotel. At present, to see anything of the B.P.'s attractions takes several weeks and expensive preparation. The former hampers the international tourist business and the latter the local resort business.

Game is the chief attraction to the tourist and Bechuanaland has an appeal to the international hunter on a variety of grounds. It is new hunting country, despite the fact that almost a century ago hunters, and later the most famous hunter in Africa, Selous, shot elephant and other game by the hundred and thousand. Elephant is not up to the East African standard, but sable and trophies of other exotic buck may be larger and many herds far more numerous.

The costs of developing hunting areas are high. To encourage a substantial investment requires protection of the investors. This means that large areas must be leased and free hunting trips through the territory by distinguished guests must not be allowed. The long-range yield from wild game also requires a close control of safari teams to ensure the best conservation practices and to avoid 'shooting out' an area. In this connection it may also be noted that game cropping could provide a valuable source of protein.

Game, like minerals, is subject to local tribal control, as well as overall Government regulation. It is not easy for a tribal *kgotla*, where the voices of illiterate old men have the greatest influence, always to reach the most sophisticated, legally and administratively sound agreements with safari companies. It has been said that the Okavango is the 'richest game land left in Africa'. Indiscriminate shooting by white tourists or by white, and more often African, poachers, already threatens the decimation of this valuable resource. In the best interests of the Batawana, the tribe most affected by hunting for game, the decisions on the development of the Okavango will have to be made at a higher administrative level than the tribal council. Suspicion of 'white' decisions from the local District Commissioner up to top Government may be finally eliminated only under African rule. But African rule is no guarantee that poaching will be effectively stopped and that wise arrangements will be entered into with outside safari companies. Meanwhile, it appears possible that new regulations can encourage investment, protect the resources, and increase the yield for the B.P. by requiring the local purchasing of supplies and employment of local inhabitants.

The second major tourist attraction, even less developed than game, is the strange and exotic life of the Bushmen described in Chapter I. The Stone Age life pattern of these 'harmless people' has a powerful fascination for many who come to know them. But there are strong local feelings, especially on the part of white officials who work closely with the Bushmen or are associated with anthropological study of them, that they should be 'left alone'. Some individuals are fiercely protective of 'my Bushmen'. Whether isolation is possible or practical is a moot point. Nevertheless it may not be impossible for wise and humane administration to allow visitors some insight into the strange, incredibly clever and fascinating life of the Bushman tribes without exploitation.

In the coming years, more expeditions and people will seek to study the Kalahari Bushmen for scientific reasons, or simply out of curiosity. Regulations to prohibit (if possible), discourage, encourage, or somehow capitalise on this interest for the benefit of the Bushmen and/or Bechuanaland will not be easy to frame, and are sure to engender fierce controversy. The 'keep them as they are' school will have as many critics among Africans generally as among people outside the continent, just as will a policy of westernising, or otherwise markedly changing their nomadic battle against the elements. One suspects that they will be settled, educated, and gradually disappear in a cultural sense from the face of the earth.

Wild animals and Bushmen do not exhaust, even though they dominate, Bechuanaland's tourist potential. One additional attraction one hesitates to mention is the famous 'lost city' of the Kalahari. But, like so many legends, it has gained a stature that no amount of debunking will destroy. One of the better 'debunking' discoveries was made by a group of Northern Rhodesian Boy Scouts. They brought back pictures of a particular geological formation which might pass for regularly shaped building blocks with mortar between them. But the legend persists. One can predict with some certainty that tourist folders will not refrain from mentioning the 'lost city', and no doubt associating it with a fabled past.

Serious tourism, whether it involves Bushmen, or shooting game with camera and gun, is just beginning in the B.P. It could provide not only welcome taxes for needed Government projects, but also employment for both unskilled and skilled Bechuanas. One would like to see the day when Bechuana-owned and managed hotels and safari companies were world famous and a major source of national revenue. That time is obviously distant, but the time to begin is at hand. The same might be said of the Okavango, perhaps Bechuanaland's greatest untapped natural resource.

Okavango

The twin natural problems of Bechuanaland are too little water and too much. The Okavango River rises in Angola, crosses the B.P. border in the extreme north-west, and discharges a large volume of water into the Okavango swamps, where it is lost through direct evaporation and evapo-transpiration of the abundant vegetation in the channels. The perenially flowing Chobe River, forming the northern border of the Protectorate and emptying into the Zambezi, has irrigation possibilities of its own.

In some years, the Okavango floods reach as far south as Lake Ngami; in others, the flood water fails to break through. In August 1963 I made an aerial reconnaissance of the lake which was then at one of the highest points in forty years and had spread out over the dry plains. Huge flights of delicately coloured pink flamingos wheeled and turned as our little plane flew low, and numerous cattle and wild animals were repeatedly threatened with isolation on low islands created by the flood waters. A century ago, David Livingstone was one of the first white men to see Lake Ngami. Although he did not go round it, he described it from hearsay as a huge inland sea with a circumference of 170 miles. The famous German geographer, Siegfried Passarge, in his 1904 study of the Kalahari, estimated the size of the lake at one time as 300 miles by 100 miles, or about the size of Lake Michigan or Lake Superior, and larger than the Irish Sea.

The Okavango delta itself has been estimated by W. G. Brind, former Director of Public Works for Bechuanaland, as embracing over 6,500 square miles, or an area almost the size of Wales. After a study in 1945, L. A. McKenzie, Director of Irrigation in South Africa, estimated that about 3,000 square miles were under water in a normal flood year. According to McKenzie, the annual rate of evaporation is 72 inches per year in the delta. Estimates of the amount of water flowing into the delta range from six to eleven million acre feet per year (an acre foot is an acre covered to a depth of one foot). By any standards, this is a tremendous volume of fresh water to be of almost no value to people living in a desert country. The obvious thought is: can one move some of the water from the swamps to the arid plains and thus make both areas more productive? To some it is a wild dream, to others a dream which will some day come true.

Most of the many water schemes in this part of Bechuanaland and in neighbouring territories are related to the flatness of the terrain. This means that exchange between river systems takes place, and that such stretches as the outlet of Lake Ngami sometimes flow one way and then turn round with a fairly stiff current in the opposite direction. Under conditions when water is spreading out over enormous areas, its movement usually becomes sluggish and thick tropical vegetation grows rapidly, impeding its flow through channels. When these clog up, the moving water finds another outlet until it, in turn, is congested with growing and dying vegetation. All of this vegetation contributes to tremendous evaporation.

Popular interest in the Okavango delta was stimulated by a famous book, *The Kalahari or Thirstland Redemption*, by E. H. L. Schwarz, published in 1920. Schwarz, Professor of Geology at Rhodes University, had been a student of the progressive dessication of Africa, and conceived a scheme whereby the swamp water was to be spread out even further through a series of lakes, and the resulting evaporation would materially improve the rainfall of much of southern Africa as far south as the Union. Subsequent studies contradicted some of Schwarz's assumptions concerning gradients, and a report in 1925 by South Africa's famous scientist, A. L. du Toit, concluded that ' the influence of increased evaporation upon the climate in South Africa would be negligible,' and recommended concentration upon irrigational aspects. Schwarz had however captured the imagination of the farming public of southern Africa, and speculation continued to be rife. A major investigation in 1945, headed by the Union Minister of Lands, Senator A. M. Conroy, led to a report by L. A. McKenzie which discounted any significant benefits for South Africa. This report seemed to kill finally the idea that climatic change could be introduced. It did not, however, rule out more limited engineering projects for irrigation in Bechuanaland. The concept now generally accepted is that the area of water should be limited and evaporation decreased rather than increased. Du Toit, Lord Hailey, Professor Debenham of Cambridge, and McKenzie, have all discussed different schemes of more limited scale. Debenham believes that some 125,000 acres in the Mababe Depression could be irrigated from the Chobe River, and another 100,000 acres irrigated along the Botletle River by diverting Okavango River water. In his *Water Resources of the Bechuanaland Protectorate*, he waxes enthusiastic, stating that given development, the Okavanga delta 'can become a second Sudan, growing cotton or other products for export under somewhat similar conditions, always provided it has reasonable access to the sea'. Prospects for the favoured rail route through South West Africa will be discussed later.

The 1960 economic survey mission appointed by Her Majesty's Government and headed by Professor Chandler Morse of Cornell University reviewed three years of practical work by W. G. Brind, and concluded that some irrigation development was immediately practicable. Looking at the region in 1964, it appears that the principal impediments to development of the Okavango delta generally fall into four categories:

1. *Scientific Information*. The need for better climatic data is obvious. The lower the rainfall, the more irregular, is a general rule. Whereas forty years may give reliable data in humid England, over a hundred years is to be preferred in dry Tanganyika (as the Groundnut Scheme showed) or Bechuanaland. What is the 'normal' size of Lake Ngami? What is the normal flow of the Chobe River? Is the apparent dessication of this part of Africa part of a progressive trend or a temporary fluctuation? Sufficient data are available on the slope of the land in the Okavango delta for minor projects to be undertaken, and also soil information is probably adequate for initial schemes such as irrigating the Mababe Depression. But great gaps remain in soil knowledge generally, and in knowledge of what can be economically grown.

2. *Engineering*. An efficient and economical method of controlling the aquatic vegetation must be found if channels are to be kept open for reasonable flow, and evapo-transpiration is to be controlled. Mechanical cutting machines are not as yet successful. Chemical control probably depends upon blocking the means of reproduction rather than

destroying existing plants. A whole new dimension has yet to be investigated in the Okavango, namely, the utilisation of vegetation for manufacture into cheap protein, as pioneered by Dr. N. W. Pirie, F.R.S., at the Rothampsted Experimental Research Station. If the waste product of cutting takes on an economic value, then the whole economics of vegetation control could be radically altered. My colleague Professor J. H. Wayland of the California Institute of Technology is optimistic that given sufficient research study, success can be achieved.

Another essential advance lies in environmental health engineering to control tsetse fly and human sickness in the Okavango. Research is under way with limited funds, and so far limited success, in Ngamiland.

3. *Transportation.* This probably means that in addition to tar roads, a railway should be built at least north from the existing system. The present atrocious road from Francistown westward is a nightmare to drive over and highly costly in vehicle repairs. The ideal rail link would be through irrigated country to a West Coast port such as Walvis Bay, or a new harbour at the mouth of Angola's Cunene River.

4. *Political.* Co-operation with neighbouring states in the collection of data and overall planning for this part of African is necessary. A major Okavango scheme is likely to require a promise of political stability.

On all scores, there is need for large sums of money for research and development. Bechuanaland will not be able to raise such funds from its own resources in the foreseeable future. Extra large sums make any project political. Will Britain wish to undertake the requisite financing for a country moving towards independence? Will a new and impoverished country be better off with the end of colonial rule and aid? Will a burgeoning Bechuanaland nationalism and eventual independence provide the initial spark and the external confidence that the United Nations, or the major world powers, would need to assist in the development of these water resources on a large scale?

Professor Darrell Randall, in his dissertation published at the University of Chicago in 1957, analyses the potential impact of Okavango development upon the lives of the local Batawana people and other human groups. He concludes that local people are simply unable to undertake responsibility for development. As a visitor to Maun, I was struck by the fact that the handful of Europeans catch more edible fish from the river than do the impoverished Africans. Yet when I talked to a group of Batawana and suggested that fish can be caught for virtually nothing, instead of spending money for meat in the market—money that could go to build the secondary school they want—a tribal council spokesman replied, 'Yes, it is easy for you to say because you know about these things, but my people won't do it if I tell them.' They will, in time, no matter how impatient Bechuanas from other parts of the country become with them for their lack of initiative, but it will take a long time at the present pace. Who is responsible for development? The lack of a firm answer, when added to the financial cost involved, is the reason development has not really begun.

Whatever the scale of the successes that may eventually attend the utilisation of the water resources of northern Bechuanaland, it is fair to conclude today that the country is unable even to finance the preliminary work required to establish sufficient confidence for large-scale study.

Transportation Infrastructure

Despite its elephantine bulk, or perhaps because of the great distances involved, Bechuanaland is remarkably poorly equipped with public transportation. It has not been economically feasible to provide an adequate road network for the scattered population. In many ways, the B.P. is highly fortunate in that it has fairly good rail service through its most densely settled region, the east, because it is traversed by the main line route from Johannesburg to Bulawayo. The ownership of this line by Rhodesian Railways makes regulation of service difficult. After considerable effort, the B.P. Administration was finally able to 'desegregate' trains and dining cars while in the Protectorate. This had not been possible when South African dining cars were used over part of the track. Although many other rail links have been proposed, some of them narrow gauge, the only financially feasible one appears to be from the present rail station of Palapye to 'Lake Dow'. The latter is actually a normally dry basin, and part of the interior drainage of the Makarikari depression. If, as proposed, a canal is built to lead Okavango River water past Maun to Lake Dow (itself a transport route), then it would probably justify being linked up with the line of rail.

Bechuanaland lacks paved highways. Graded level roads cover about 1,200 miles, but the bulk of the 4,500 miles of 'road' in the territory are merely tracks. Travel in four-wheeled vehicles is often hampered or blocked by very rough surfaces, loose sand, or flash floods. The Ghanzi block in the west is more easily reached by 180 miles to the railhead in South West Africa than the 400 dusty road miles from Lobatsi. The road westward to Maun is occasionally impassable. Public transport over these limited and inferior roads is poor, and a sense of isolation affects both farmers and administrators. The loan to Bechuanaland of £1.3 million by the World Bank's International Development Association, for road communications including twelve bridges, will permit a substantial improvement in road conditions on several heavily travelled roads. The whole country has nine service stations for vehicles. Telegraph and telephone service has improved, but is still poor. Short-wave radios are an essential item, heavily relied upon by safari companies, service stations, the airline, police, and general administration. Air travel is almost too expensive for the administration of such a poor country, and there are no products which can pay for air freight.

The major travel improvement in recent years was the launching of a regular air service in Lobatsi by Captain Herbert Bartaune. Operating three small Piper aircraft, and with two other pilots, Bartaune has provided thrice weekly or weekly flights to all principal points of the protectorate. It has made possible weekly meetings of the Executive Council, the rapid evacuation of many sick or injured people from places lacking hospitals or even a doctor, and permits key civil servants to visit field projects for first-hand study without losing an inordinate amount of time away from headquarters. It is difficult to assess the financial savings and greater efficiency promoted by this fledgling airline, but its favourable impact is noticeable throughout the territory. Scarce medical and technical personnel are used far more widely and at lower salary cost for work accomplished through periodic visits to remote points.

One factor not officially calculated upon in weighing up the pros and cons of the necessary Government subsidy of the airline is its role in stimulating national consciousness. Particularly in Ghanzi and in Maun, I found that educated and semi-educated people had gained a feeling of being far closer to other parts of the country. A sense of remoteness and often resulting antagonism for the Administration has been lessened by the regular flights. The airline, now operated by a Pretoria firm, does not directly affect the great majority of inhabitants, but indirectly it is making a major contribution to the sense of a Bechuana nation.

Among the private fliers in the B.P. is Wenela, the company which recruits for the gold mines of the Witwatersrand and Free State gold fields. Wenela actually controls the Francistown airfield and operates the largest equipment regularly flown in the territory, a DC-3 which flies recruits, many of them who have come south from Angola, out to the Maun airport. It was on the Wenela airfield that an East African DC-3 was sabotaged and burned in 1963.

The cost of aircraft operation in Bechuanaland is much lower than it otherwise would be because of the excellent overhaul facilities and spares depot available in Pretoria and at Jan Smuts airports in the Republic. Various South African private companies have bid to operate subsidised services in the B.P. Civil control of the headquarters would then rest with the Republican authorities, although operations in Bechuanaland would have to comply with Protectorate laws.

Finance and Planning

Bechuanaland has been slow to develop for many reasons already outlined. Total Government revenue in 1948 was under £5 million. Grants-in-aid from the U.K. began in 1956 and rose until they now account for one-third of a budget in excess of £18 million. The B.P.'s share of customs income with South Africa for 1962-63 is estimated at £280,000. The B.P., even more than most colonial territories, had been left for decades to try to raise itself by its bootstraps. Today, its social and economic stirring is directly attributable to grants and loans from the British Government. It is not likely that Great Britain would continue to make up a major annual deficit in an independent country, nor is it likely that other foreign powers will assume a regular subsidy burden. Thus, financing becomes a major barrier to independence to a degree that scarcely existed for most newly-independent former British territories in Africa. As the Economic Survey Mission put it bluntly in 1960, without a marked improvement in the economy there is no prospect that the Protectorate revenues can suffice unaided to meet its ordinary recurrent expenditures on the bare minimum of public services. Unless there is economic development, there can be no full and stable independence.

The 1963-68 Bechuanaland Development Plan is the first comprehensive and carefully worked out effort to list targets and the means whereby they can be met. It involves the expenditure of over £12,000,000, of which a quarter is to be spent on the stimulation of production and exports. But the plan has inherent limitations. In the planners' own words, 'In the absence of a statistical organisation, which in most countries enables planners to attempt a more detailed diagnosis of economic problems, to set quantitative targets and to evaluate past programmes exactly, a pragmatic approach has to be adopted towards development planning in Bechuanaland.'

The plan called for £11,279,000 in external aid. Local taxes are to be used, but their revenue-generating potential is extremely low. Stimulation in the private sector is stressed. The primary assistance is through development of infrastructure. But in conditioning the mass of the population to economic growth, the Government is actively at work on such a key issue as land tenure reform. Various loan schemes are in operation and a National Development Bank is envisaged. Tax concessions to attract foreign capital are also viewed in a favourable light.

External trade has not been easy to balance for the B.P., and the value of imports has run some 20 per cent higher than the value of exports, or an unfavourable balance of the order of £500,000, in recent years. This is, of course, natural for a developing country spending grant and loan money, and the problems of credit are not serious while Bechuanaland remains within the British ambit. However, an independent African Government would now face staggering problems in its trade balance, credit, and in its currency, if the last were not tied to sterling. If it is not possible to reduce the £500,000 spent on vehicles each year or to manufacture locally much of the £1,500,000 worth of general merchandise, an African Government in exchange difficulties would very likely attempt to cut down on the £500,000 worth of imported grain and grain meal by growing more grain locally and by substituting locally grown produce. Fertiliser, which has been accounting for under £100,000 in annual imports, is sure to rise in importance and will climb rapidly if a crash programme of local grain production gets under way. The point is again obvious: these imports are relatively inexpensive for value received by world standards because they are bought on the low-priced South African market. Alternative and more distant sources of supply could raise prices exorbitantly.

Internal political considerations are important in the development plan. The argument is advanced that increases in the regular Government budget are undesirable in that the creation of a permanently unbalanced budget would be a crippling imposition upon an independent Government. There is no easy way out for the British Government. If it does give large sums, their withdrawal will upset an African Government; if they are continued, it will be neo-colonialism; and if additional funds are not given either time, the charge of neglect will hold water. This conundrum arises not only from current financial policies, but because Bechuanaland, along with Basutoland and Swaziland, was terribly neglected in the long pre-World War II period when the whole concept of aiding undeveloped territories with outside financing was not yet generally accepted.

Political factors also dictate the announced priority of education over medicine. The very real role of education in medical improvements is evident in such diseases as tuberculosis, where the barrier in the B.P. is not medical knowledge but an inability of the patients and their families to understand and carry out instructions.

The cost of the Gaberones capital will account for one-fifth of expenditure under the plan. This high proportion is defended on the grounds that the creation of a national symbol is essential to the primacy of national interests over purely tribal ones, in turn a prerequisite of economic growth. Furthermore, the Africanisation of the civil service, first politically and in turn economically desirable, was not really feasible at Mafeking, Cape Province. If any part of the development costs is underestimated, it is likely to be the creation of the new capital.

The 1963–68 plan is the first real effort to involve non-British financial resources in assisting Government schemes. The principal appeal is to the United Nations for help in research on hydrology, tsetse, fauna, livestock, and education. Actual work is envisioned in rural literacy, in conducting a census, giving agricultural credit, and in road building. Modest help is also budgeted for from the Oxford Committee for Famine Relief and the Freedom from Hunger Campaign. But the bulk of financial aid will continue to come from the United Kingdom Government.

The Development Plan envisages local revenue as being only slightly greater than grant-in-aid in the early years of the plan, but that by 1967–68, local revenues will have increased some 80 per cent, while the grant-in-aid will have dropped 10 per cent. That is a long time to look ahead in Bechuanaland, and the planners stress the need for yearly adjustments in their estimates and goals. It is really not so much a five-year plan as a rolling plan for the next five years, readjusted annually.

The B.P. plan is fairly straightforward in attempting to apply some oil to all parts of a creaky economic machine, and to increase both income from cattle and the education of the people. Almost no money is planned for totally new directions of development. The planned research on peasant farm units must precede any major expenditures. With such a limited budget, a major effort cannot be made on the Okavango Scheme. Here it is hoped that the United Nations or even outside private investment will lend a hand with what can be an extremely expensive and potentially extremely rewarding avenue of development.

In the final analysis, the colonial power governing a poor country such as Bechuanaland is wise not to risk its small competence on major gambles, but instead to move ahead more slowly but safely with the host of pedestrian projects such as dispensaries, small dams, land surveying, schools, roads and veterinary services. Heavy pressures on an African Government for spectacular advances may develop with autonomy. If a Government is duly elected by the people and there is national consensus to follow a risky, if potentially rewarding, path, then an African Government can do this without the same political dangers, or as bitter recriminations, as if a colonial Government gambled and lost. If Britain can continue to make up for years of neglect and in time turn over an improving country with revenue and expenses as nearly balanced as possible, it will have produced a base of action for African leadership. What financial help an African Government will attract from the world or closer at home from already independent African states is not easily predictable. Nor is it easy to fortell how successful it may be in igniting a national spirit among its own people to march forward economically.

IV. BECHUANALAND'S EXTERNAL RELATIONS

STRATEGICALLY, Bechuanaland is one of the most important countries on the African continent. That is an assertion rather than accepted fact, but the evidence to support it is impressive.

At the 1963 General Assembly of the United Nations, it was the view of the American delegation that in the sudden absence of cold war tension, and apart from Cuba, the Middle East and the question of mainland China's membership, the four most important issues all lay in southern Africa, to wit: Southern Rhodesia, Angola, South West Africa and South Africa. All these countries have major borders with Bechuanaland except for Angola, whose border is only thirty miles away across sparsely inhabited territory. An independent Bechuanaland would mean that, for the first time, a free African nation had a common border with South Africa. (The contact between Northern Rhodesia and South West Africa or the remote Caprivi Strip has nothing like the strategic importance of Bechuanaland, whose longer border is close to the huge population centres and vital industry of the Witwatersrand.)

If there is major guerrilla warfare or unconditional military fighting between the Pan-African states and the Republic, the easiest approach from the north is through the B.P. On the other hand, the openness of the country and lack of cover militates against surprise and concealment such as would be possible on other borders, particularly that of Mozambique, with the Republic.

With or without armed conflict on the borders of Bechuanaland, the role of the Protectorate will loom importantly in the debates of the United Nations. In the absence of overriding threats to world peace, the wishes of the largest continental *bloc* at the United Nations, which constitutes a third of its membership, will have a high priority at future meetings of the General Assembly. If nothing else unites the diverse leadership of the newly-independent states of Africa, they are drawn together by a dislike of a system of government which appears to be based upon a belief in the superiority of a white skin over a dark skin, regardless of any other factor. Granted the pressures which will exist at the United Nations, and assuming that South Africa continues to appear intransigent and Portugal somewhat less so, the most obvious target for effective pressure will be the United Kingdom. In most recent sessions, Rhodesia has often held the spotlight, not because African nations felt it was more important than South Africa, but because the opportunities of applying effective pressures were so much greater. Just as South West Africa is judged the most effective way of closing in on South Africa, so pressure on the U.K. over Bechuanaland may be the most effective way of further involving Britain in the southern Africa struggle.

It is not unlikely that one or more individual events in Bechuanaland—involving Pan-African revolutionary elements and the South African Government—will become the focus for a major debate in the United Nations. Not only would the nations in Africa be aligned on one side or the other, but the whole galaxy of world powers on opposite sides of the cooling war—the U.S.S.R., the U.S., and the neutralist *bloc*—would be included. In the wings, Red China would stand prepared to take advantage of any Soviet hesitancy in adopting a militant position. The claim that South West Africa at present represents a threat to world peace would have the same degree of validity as some kinds of political tension in Bechuanaland.

Thus, it appears that Bechuanaland, the subject of whose external relations would have been as dry as Kalahari dust a decade ago, has a strategic significance far beyond her population or economic strength.

Relations with South Africa

The outstanding facts from the long history of Bechuanaland's relations with the Republic are Britain's understanding with South Africa that eventually the territory would become part of South Africa, and Britain's commitment to the Bechuana people that any change of sovereignty would not take place without their consent. It is not conceivable that any foreseeable British Government would honour the first promise at the price of dishonouring the second.

However, that is not to say that Bechuanas will not continue to fear such an eventuality. Certainly, those fears will be exploited and played upon for diverse political ends.

They were once again aroused on 3 September 1963, by a speech by Prime Minister Hendrik F. Verwoerd in Pretoria. The South African Premier began his first extensive public comment on the High Commission Territories by good neighbourly remarks and, surprisingly, mentioned both the Ganyile and Abrahams cases. In the former, South African police had crossed into Basutoland a few yards further than was their legal right to kidnap a suspect and maintained their innocence for eighteen months before releasing the African politician with compensation. The later and better known case of kidnapping was carried out inside Bechuanaland by South African police from South West Africa in civilian clothes, and it was generally accepted that they were acting on their own with excessive zeal. Dr. Verwoerd acknowledged these mistakes and pointed to the rectification made by releasing both men. He then complained about the use of South African airspace between Swaziland and Bechuanaland as an escape route. He described what he was trying to do in the Transkei as similar to Britain's objectives in the Protectorates.

Prime Minister Verwoerd reaffirmed that his Government had no territorial ambitions and continued, 'Indeed, were they under our guardianship, South Africa would free them stage by stage, just as she is doing in the Transkei.'

He then outlined what South Africa would do if it had responsibility for the High Commission territories. He would make them 'democratic states in which the masses would not be dominated by small groups of authoritarians'. He would steer them 'away from the principle of multi-racism' and give the whites who remained a vote in South Africa. He would also exchange certain areas at present in the Protectorate for others now lying within the Republic, and said this would be of primary advantage to Africans. Lastly, he would apply the border industries concept in South Africa to the High Commission Territories, so that while political rule would be in African hands, much of the African employment would be across the border in South African factories.

There followed his 'challenge' to Great Britain to allow the inhabitants of the territories to decide whose assistance they preferred.

The world Press reacted with great swiftness and heat. Its general line was that South Africa was again trying to put into effect the original understanding that it would eventually take over the territorites. Many commentators implied the use of military force. Copies of Dr. Verwoerd's remarks were not available, and the world Press was dependent upon the hasty notes of local newsmen at the time he spoke. In an effort to catch up with the first stories, a statement was issued two days later in Pretoria. It emphasised that 'no offer was made to the United Kingdom to "annex" or "take over" or "incorporate" or "administer" these territories.' It underlined Britain's responsibility to consult the inhabitants before making any changes such as would lead to the Republic's being a 'guide and guardian'. The Prime Minister emphasised that incorporation 'was not sought since this was against my Government's policy of separate development which has as its objective the political independence of the Bantu nation'. He also declared that those who would deny South Africa the chance to put its case to the people of the territories were exposing their 'fear' of truth.

In part, the proposals were genuinely misunderstood, but in even greater part, some critics of South Africa seized upon the statement as one which they could twist to make political capital. The whole affair revealed a profound underestimation of world opinion on the part of Dr. Verwoerd's advisers and a misjudgment of Press reaction. Had such an essentially economic proposal—whatever the political motivations behind it—been set forth clearly and unequivocally in a major policy statement, copies of which would have been available to journalists in South Africa and through South African embassies abroad, and possibly even through some full-page newspaper advertisements such as were used for the Transkei announcements, then the criticism would have been more of what actually was said and less of what the commentators expected would have been said.

Although the issue has been raised in the United Nations, the practical political consequences of South Africa taking over Bechuanaland by military force in any situation short of war between South Africa and Pan-African states are such as to make the move highly unlikely. Nothing would give South Africa's foes greater pleasure than for the Republic to make an overt and aggressive move outside its own borders. Many nations, particularly those in Western Europe, who share a repugnance for racial discrimination, are inhibited from action against South Africa because of a deep conviction that they would be interfering in the internal politics of a sovereign nation. All moral reservations could be swept away if South Africa were to seize Bechuanaland.

Similar considerations operate against South Africa's military assistance to the white minority Governments of Southern Rhodesia and Angola. South Africa has a vital stake in the Portuguese achieving a *modus vivendi* with

African nationalism and thus protecting South Africa's flanks in Angola and Mozambique. But, despite South Africa's interest in helping the hard-pressed Portuguese, the military assistance has been almost nil. A few planeloads of small arms were sent secretly to Angola in the early days of the revolt, but nothing approaching the kind of aid the United States gives to many nations with which it is only lukewarm friends, or the kind of military equipment the Soviet Union and Red China supply to countries only peripherally affecting their own policies.

Diplomatic statements must obviously be analysed as to whether they make sense to the country concerned. A senior South African diplomat's comment to the writer, that if South Africa took over Bechuanaland it would make a farce of the Bantustan policy, has a logic consistent with South Africa's stated goals. As he pointed out, 'South Africa is engaged in a policy of spinning off territories with a large African population. The Transkei is far from independent in 1964, but the trend towards some measure of autonomy for various African-settled parts of the Republic is undeniable. This is true even if one is convinced that such areas are not economically viable or that independence for them is no solution to the political demands of millions of Africans in the so-called "white areas".'

Any attempt to slow up even limited autonomy, or the drastic step of acquiring peacefully by treaty, or of physically seizing additional territory with an African majority, makes no sense at all if there is a shred of sincerity in the Bantustan programme. This is an argument based on the theory of separate development. In fact, and a number of leading South African officials will put this point privately, the exact opposite is the case; the High Commission Territories, and perhaps Bechuanaland in particular, are essential to making South Africa's case. The reasoning is as follows: pressures are building up against the Republic and it will be some years before the Transkei could really be indepen-dent. In the Transkei development, South Africa will be in a dilemma between giving political control to a poor and woefully backward (if potentially highly productive) agricultural region, and pouring in many millions of Rand as she is now doing to raise the economic level, but postponing any real independence because of the economic dependence created. It is doubtful if the Transkei could generate 25 per cent of its internal financial needs within five years. The rest is at present coming from the South African taxpayer, and some of that tax money represents the sweat from the brow of migrant Xhosa from the Transkei. Thus, the interrelationship will continue for some time and fail to allow the world actually to judge—for sure—whether or not South Africa is sincere about its separate development or Bantustan programme.

This is where Bechuanaland enters behind the scenes in South African thinking. No one has any doubts that Great Britain and not South Africa has political control in the B.P. Even if there has to be outside financial assistance to Bechuanaland, it is still possible for that country to achieve independence in a few years. The Bechuanas may insist upon financial links which could, in some ways, appear to limit their independence. However, such links would probably be less limiting than those accompanying South Africa's economic aid and retention of political controls in the Transkei and in subsequent Bantustans.

It is against this background that South African statements regarding the B.P. must be viewed. Bechuanaland could become, in South African thinking, an independent African state bordering on South Africa and benefiting materially from close economic ties. If South Africa were thus able to help finance such an African state and to maintain normal diplomatic relations with it, there would be far less doubt about her ability to grant similar status to large parts of South Africa where overwhelming African populations are located.

Such a development would, of course, require a drastic revision of present South African official and private attitudes towards African diplomats. Various pro-Government newspapers, led by *Die Burger* in Cape Town, and often followed up by *Dagbreek en Sondagnuus* (Chairman of the Board, Dr. Verwoerd) in Johannesburg, have been insisting for a long time that South Africa must receive African diplomats from the Transkei, as well as from other parts of Africa, with precisely the same degree of courtesy and non-segregated facilities as are accorded any other diplomats. The necessity for this is widely recognised among senior members of the South African Government, and particularly among its diplomats.

The obvious question an outsider asks is: 'Why, if Africans enjoying diplomatic status and even businessmen from outside South Africa can be treated on the basis of merit and not colour, cannot this same treatment be applied to all Africans with similar education and cultural values within the country?' The answer lies less in racial feeling than in power politics. It is often overlooked that at heart the Afrikaner nationalist is far less interested in oppressing than he is determined not to be oppressed. The great thrust of his history has been to overthrow British colonialism—including neo-colonialism—and petty discrimination. As Minister of Defence Jim Fouche told his Bloemfontein constituents in 1963, 'In the world today one race cannot dominate another race.' It is precisely the power aspects which would create a situation of equal treatment for an African diplomat but less than equal treatment of a local African professor, though even the latter's position might possibly be improved by the change of attitude towards the diplomat.

If this has a cuckooland quality to it, one must recall that a strikingly similar situation still persists in the United States today. When large numbers of African diplomats began arriving in Washington and for the United Nations in New York, they were soon able to go into residential areas, restaurants, and other public facilities from which Americans of African descent were barred. They still have an advantage in most parts of the American South. It is an often repeated stunt for an American Negro who can speak French or Spanish to put on a turban and robes to gain access to many places in the southern states where he could not gain admission in a grey flannel suit. It was Komla Gbedemah, then Minister of Finance in Ghana, who deliberately broke the colour bar in some Howard Johnson restaurants in Maryland by precipitating a famous incident over a glass of orange juice.

The parallel of African diplomats gradually gaining acceptance for all people of colour is conceivable in South Africa. Indeed, the thought is used with a reverse twist by some racists in South Africa as a reason for resisting the proposed non-discriminatory treatment of African diplomats. I have travelled in South Africa with fellow Americans of African descent and stayed at the best hotels, etc., without anything but the most courteous treatment, although this is most unusual. The change would not be so great as might be imagined.

The official Bechuanaland Government position *vis-à-vis* South Africa was defined as one of 'strictest neutrality' in the interests of 'a vigourous and uncompromising advance towards an independent, stable, prosperous and non-racial state', in the words of the Queen's Commissioner Peter Fawcus to the B.P. Legislature in November, 1963. He described the policy as 'a counsel of caution but not of timidity'. Refererring to those 'with whom we must trade if we are to live', he pointed to the wisdom that has been 'learned by all the small nations which have succeeded in preserving their independence in the modern world'. The statement on external affairs was possible because of the change of title of the Resident Commissioner to that of Her Majesty's Commissioner with the status of a Governor.

Mr. Fawcus commented further *inter alia*:

I have been left in no doubt during recent months that the strong determination of responsible people in Bechuanaland is that the territory shall not become a mere pawn in international politics, or an instrument for any action against other territories, because the people of the territory have more important and more rewarding things to do for themselves.

At the same time Bechuanaland will continue to give asylum to persons who if they return to South Africa would face loss of liberty as a consequence of political opinion or acts expressed or performed before they left South Africa.

In this we shall be upholding the traditions and beliefs of Bechuanaland as well as of Great Britain.

Mr. Fawcus's declared policy provided the justification for the refusal of political asylum to three South West African leaders, who had been living in Tanganyika and who sought to enter Bechuanaland from Northern Rhodesia. In March 1964, Mr. Sam Nujoma, Mr. Jacob Kahangua and Mr. Emil Appolus arrived, they said to make arrangements for refugees from South West Africa now in Bechuanaland to proceed to Dar es Salaam. The three men had no passports or travel documents and refused to be fingerprinted as the immigrants law requires.

Most of the foregoing discussion of South Africa and Bechuanaland relations anticipates a larger role for local leadership in Bechuanaland. Present political relationships are between South Africa and Great Britain. But let us shift our vantage point to the B.P. itself and consider the attitudes of the two major parties to the Republic. Their differences on this question are probably the deepest ones which divide them. The Bechuanaland Democratic Party's attitude to the Republic certainly accounts in large part for how the various class and racial groups line up. If this attitude does not change, it may well be that a majority of the Pan-African states will support the Bechuanaland People's Party rather than the B.D.P., in so far as they concern themselves with the internal politics of Bechuanaland.

One could step back from the political heat of the South African attitudes and say with perhaps greater truth that the Democratic Party is more concerned with the economic life of the territory and with raising its living standards and less concerned with anti-British feeling (assuming independence is round the corner in any case) or even anti-South African actions on behalf of a broader African cause. The People's Party has not had time, in Matante's words, 'to think about our economic policy'. His opponent, Quett Masire, has been effective at political meetings by saying that his party was interested in what was best for Bechuanaland—not what some outside (African) politicians wanted Bechuanaland to do for them. On joining with South Africa, Masire says, 'South Africa and the High Commission Territories have reached a point of no return in the respective courses they have chosen. It is a well known fact that the Republic and ourselves are poles apart.'

The attitude of Seretse Khama, Masire, and the Democratic Party generally towards South Africa is to criticise severely, in plain fact to abhor, policies involving discrimination on the basis of race. But there is no 'Black Muslim' justification for segregation. Likewise, the official British position is absolutely against any form of racial bias and a good many individual officials go much further than the official line in their criticism of Republican policies. But when it comes to non-political matters, the Democratic leaders soberly point out over and over again the financial advantages now accruing to the territory from present economic arrangements with the Republic. These not only include favourable customs arrangements (and here Swaziland probably is at a disadvantage), but the host of small yet significant technical relationships referred to earlier. For example, the Republic veterinary laboratory furnishes a great deal of free advice and serums for Bechuanaland, as it does for some independent African states. If an African or European has an unusual or severe illness, there are African and European medical specialists available only a few hours away in Johannesburg. Bechuanaland has no medical specialists, nor even a single dentist, for that matter. Technical experts in such diverse subjects as well drilling, short-wave radio repair and crystallography are available nearby at low cost.

Although South Africa is gradually reducing the numbers of workers it will admit from neighbouring territories, and complaints are coming from Bechuanas about employment doors closing, the monthly receipts of workers in the Republic play a significant role in territorial finances, not to mention the acquisition of skills. South Africa is the largest wage employer of Bechuanas, and it furnishes the bulk of skilled personnel to the Protectorate. Access to the sea for critical exports, as well as most normal import routes, is through Cape Town's docks.

South Africa is an important supplier of Bechuanaland's needs and especially of unusual services at relatively low cost. Conversely, South Africa needs Bechuanaland labour or would suffer temporary dislocation in gold mining without it. The B.P. is a good market for South Africa's secondary industries, and South Africa makes a good middleman profit on much that is imported to Bechuanaland.

But the economic balance, a force unrelated to political rights and wrongs, is overwhelmingly on the side of South Africa. It underlines the force of the dilemma that any nation or group of nations who wish to break Bechuanaland's ties with South Africa must offer immediate economic succour, or ask the Bechuanas to pay a heavy price in human suffering. Poverty is a constant cousin to most Bechuanas. Wise chiefs still require three years storage of grain before allowing a surplus to be sold. But no chiefs have the financial resources among their people to withstand the cessation of human and trade intercourse between the two countries unless major assistance is forthcoming.

But what of the legal position between the two countries? Under South African law, Bechuanaland has been a foreign territory for travel purposes since July 1963 under provisions of the Commonwealth Relations Bill of 1962. Great Britain is directly involved with South Africa on behalf of the High Commission Territories in the question of air rights. The fairly frequent use of Swaziland and Basutoland as havens for refugees has often been followed by clandestine charter flights across South Africa to Bechuanaland. In a few instances, particularly the flight of Patrick Duncan from Basutoland to Bechuanaland, the South African police probably had an advance tip-off, and the South African air force could have intercepted the twin-engine Piper aircraft if such an act had been called for.[1] After later refugee flights, South Africa unilaterally barred overflights and threatened to revoke the licenses of the local air operators who had been doing refugee flying. Access to the Basutoland enclave is not barred, but planes must land in the Republic. This is South Africa's right under the Chicago Convention. South African fighters have forced down a plane from Basutoland which at first ignored instructions.

At what point might South Africa ring down an iron curtain on the B.P. boundary? There has been occasional provocation—more in statements than legally. Bechuanaland's Government has insisted that refugees—all of whom are welcomed—will not stand in Bechuanaland and literally or figuratively fire into the Republic. South Africa will gradually build up more fences and heavier patrols of the border to prevent wanted saboteurs or political organisers from escaping, just as it will attempt to control more closely the influx of guerrilla weapons and those who would organise revolt.

On balance, South Africa is unlikely to be provoked into a hasty closing down of the Bechuanaland border. Such a move would cast Bechuanaland adrift to fend economically for itself and almost inevitably it would then become an armed base against the Republic with or without British

[1] Duncan, the son of the first South African-born Governor General, was the founder and for a long time the Editor of *Contact* magazine; he was also a prominent member of the South African Liberal Party. He left South Africa on a British passport and without an exit permit at a time when an order was in force against him under the Suppression of Communism Act, confining him to Cape Town for five years.

acquiescence. World opinion would notch up another black mark against South Africa and, more important in political terms, white South Africans would feel a sense of isolation and of retreat behind an uncertain barrier. South Africa has a trump card in its essential and, indeed, generous economic support of Bechuanaland, but a trump can only be played once, and then it is gone.

South West Africa

If, as is often suggested, Bechuanaland is not economically viable, the question arises of its association with other states. The links discussed with South Africa are economically the most logical, and politically the least likely. A tie with South West Africa has seldom been considered for the obvious reason that both territories are desperately poor and undeveloped. However, South West Africa today has one of the best potentials in Africa for a high *per capita* income. Considered as a separate country from the Republic, with the world's richest diamond mines and off-shore recovery, the booming fishing and canning industry, the success of karakul (Persian Lamb) ranching, the unique Tsumeb ore body, the finds of semi-precious stones, and the mainstay cattle industry, South West Africa is moderately wealthy. Most of the capital is external, and most of the profits are sent outside South West Africa, but even when that is taken into account, the prospects for the relatively small population (500,000) are excellent.

Both South West and the B.P. are sparsely settled, and, along with Mauritania, have the lowest population density in Africa. Vegetationally, both are cattle countries and populated by cattle tribes. Africans are not the only cattle people there; the livelihood of a majority of Europeans in both territories is intimately associated with livestock. Bechuanaland is probably capable of a considerable expansion in meat exports, as various U.K. commissions have concluded. If one examines a map showing areas within fifty miles of the southern and eastern borders of the B.P., one is immediately struck by the far greater ranching development on the South and South West Africa sides of the border, under the same climatic conditions. It would seem technically feasible, putting racial issues aside for the moment, that skilled management in South West Africa could take the lead in expanding the B.P. livestock industry.

A second area of mutual interest between South West Africa and the B.P. is transport. We have seen how the Ghanzi block has partially changed its orientation from Gobabis in South West Africa to Lobatsi. But, as I have suggested, it is conceivable that the whole of Bechuanaland would be most efficiently linked with the outside world by a rail line to Walvis Bay.

The 1952 British mission to investigate the possibilities of economic development in the Western Kalahari[1] were in favour of a southerly route from the present railhead at Gobabis in South West Africa to Lobatsi. An alternative route, first surveyed in 1931 by Mr. Jeffares of Rhodesian Railways, strikes northwest from Ghanzi to reach the Rhodesian line just south of Livingstone. The route would serve Ngamiland and the northern B.P., while in no way duplicating the existing line from Lobatsi to Francistown, and west to Bulawayo. An obvious advantage to Zambia of a west coast port for goods destined for Europe lies in the great saving of distance around southern Africa from Beira.

A proposal in late 1963 by the London firm of Lonrho envisaged a £20 million coal-by-pipe project from the Wankie Collieries in Rhodesia across northern Bechuanaland to South West Africa. The company already has extensive land and mining holdings in central Africa. A spokesman expected that four million tons of granulated coal a year could be flushed through the pipe each year by using one million gallons of water every day. The coal would be used to produce power at the American-owned Tsumeb mine, and would then carry on to the Atlantic coast. The

---

[1] The members were A. Gaitskell, C. U. Pickrell, B. Curry, Tshekedi Khama, Bathoen II, and L. van der Post.

intensive South African efforts to develop northern South West Africa economically may lead to the exploitation of an iron ore deposit estimated at 200 million tons in the Kaokoveld, and the building of a new Atlantic seaport. The proposed pipeline could, with considerable difficulty, be routed through the Caprivi Strip, but northern Bechuanaland would be a far more likely route.

Other possible developments than those proposed by Lonrho would also involve an Atlantic port and a rail link across northern B.P. All such proposals would lead to closer economic association of the two cattle countries.

The practical difficulties of construction of either the northern or southern trans-Kalahari line are not insuperable. Walvis Bay has had £5,000,000 in new railway facilities and steady harbour expansion. The line from the port to Windhoek would need heavier rails and ballast for increased traffic. For the new construction, hills, curves, sand, and rivers are not major obstacles. Experts anticipate that adequate water would be found, and its presence is less critical in railway technology than when such a route was first proposed.

The question of traffic potential from Zambia and Rhodesia is involved with political questions which we will come to shortly. Northern Bechuanaland would be much closer to Walvis Bay than to Cape Town. No one can foretell with certainty the political future of South West Africa. If it were independent, and agreed to construction of a Kalahari route, then the B.P. would find itself free of dependence upon the South African Railways. However, any such speculation must also take into account that in law Walvis Bay is not at present part of South West Africa, but an enclave of the Cape Province, and thus part of the Republic of South Africa proper. Whatever World Court and United Nations decisions are made about South West Africa, technically they would not apply to the harbour of Walvis Bay. It is not however the only possible South West African harbour terminus for a Kalahari railway.

Kalahari lions will kill many thousands of buck before some of these speculations are proved true or otherwise, but they are not far-fetched. Recently, the leader of the South West Africa People's Organisation, Dr. Mburumba Kerina, was staying for some weeks at the home of Vice-President Matante of the Bechuanaland People's Party in Francistown, following many world travels and frequent petitions at the United Nations. They each told me of their long discussions on the possible joining of their two countries when and if each of them gained political power.

Tsumeb-born Kerina left South West Africa in 1953, and is under threat of arrest on South African soil. He returned to the vicinity of South West Africa with his American wife and children with the announced intention of proceeding to South West Africa. Whether Kerina, having returned from visits to many parts of the Communist and non-Communist worlds, and particularly from the United Nations, is technically a refugee from South West Africa, was not immediately clear to the Bechuanaland Administration.

With this must be linked the presence in Ngamiland of a large number of Hereros. These are the flourishing descendants (in most cases) of Hereros who fled South West Africa in pre-World War I days of German authority, after General von Trotha issued his infamous order that the Hereros must be 'exterminated'. Despite more than a generation in exile, sentiment runs strongly for return to South West Africa. The Hereros are a potential source of trouble in Bechuanaland, but not because of irredentist tendencies. They simply want to return home, and are a potential source of embarrassment between the South African and British Governments. Britain cannot seem to encourage a group of Africans to move voluntarily under South African control, and the South Africans are not sure where they would put the homecomers without displacing other indigenous Southwesters. Even if the two countries were united, the desire to return to their 'homeland' would probably be as strong. The Hereros that the writer interviewed around Maun seemed to care far more for a sense of tribe and tribal homeland than the flag flying over the local police station. On the other hand, the writer gained the impression from a long meeting with the Herero patriarch, Chief Hosea Kutako, and his councillors in Windhoek, that they preferred a closer tribal link with the Ngamiland Hereros rather than their physical return.

Bechuanaland's borders with South West Africa involve the territory in the whole question of the United Nations attempting to impose its conclusion upon the South African Government. If a point of physical confrontation is reached, Great Britain might well be asked to co-operate with the United Nations in allowing access through Bechuanaland. This issue arose once before when a peaceful United Nations group under Professor Fabregat of Uruguay wished to visit South West Africa. They were refused entry by the South African authorities and were reported to have considered crossing the border from Bechuanaland. The writer was in Windhoek at the time (1960) and discovered that the airport control tower did have instructions to allow a United Nations plane to land, rather than risk a crash if it ran out of fuel.

At the time of the committee's visit, Britain was hesitant to allow Bechuanaland to become involved. South Africa intensified police coverage along the B.P. border and, in the end, the mission did not venture beyond Southern Rhodesia.

The physical border is not physiographically significant. Although previously agreed, it was first demarcated by German and British teams working in 1902 and 1903. The account of the marking of the boundary, contained in the German military publication, *Militar Wochenblatt*, in 1913, is one of hardship and perseverance by both parties against dangerous odds imposed by nature. The Boer War was an additional hazard for the British, and an Herero uprising killed 18 of the German commission.

More recently, the South Africans have checked the boundary and found only a few hundred yards of error, a remarkable tribute to the Germans, considering that they depended upon the accuracy of watches brought up from the coast with an error of less than a second. The border is fenced, originally to control game. However, South Africa has been strengthening the fencing round all the High Commission Territories since leaving the Commonwealth. The fence is sturdy, but sections are occasionally knocked down by large herds of animals such as wildebeest, who encounter it running across open country, and are unable to stop until the mass has forced its way through with casualties. The South African surveyors have themselves crossed it by pulling out enough posts for parts of the fence to flatten on the ground, allowing a truck to be driven through.

Physical control along the entire South West Africa and B.P. borders would require large numbers of troops. On the other hand, surveillance is not difficult in the open country, and South Africa may well utilise some new helicopters as an economical form of 'fence-riding'. The Abrahams escape and subsequent kidnapping later discussed, showed how easy it was to move either way at that time. The new alertness would probably make both manoeuvres much harder to repeat, after years in which the border meant little to anyone except the occasional African cattle smuggler. South Africa has refused to accept Bechuanaland beef on the hoof, giving fear of foot and mouth disease as the reason. This is already an endemic problem in South West Africa. Measures to control smuggling may thus be aimed either at cattle or at political suspects, and it is not always easy to distinguish between them.

At the 1963 session of the Legislative Council, Mr. T. T. Tsheko of Ngamiland stirred support for his motion that Bechuanaland should take over the Caprivi Strip. Some of the 20,000 Africans in the 15,000 square miles of desert, scrubland, and swamp are Bechuanas, although the majority are Mpukushu. It is certainly a trading point between the B.P. Government and South Africa as the administering power for South West Africa. If Bechuanaland acquired the Caprivi, it would gain broader access to Zambia and, a valuable point in decades to come, a common border with Angola.

Rhodesia (Southern Rhodesia)

Southern Rhodesia's special interest in the Tati Concession, the desire of some white farmers in the Tati to join with Rhodesia, the use hitherto of Bulawayo as the major shopping city for northeastern Bechuanaland, and the ownership of the railroad through the B.P., are not of great significance in forming African attitudes. One is unable to find Africans who would wish that their part of the B.P. were annexed to Rhodesia.

On the other hand, in discussions with Matabele in the Bulawayo area, some of them seemed not averse to re-establishing the Matabele hegemony of Lobengula in the last century over much of northern Bechuanaland. It is well within the realm of possibility that a predominantly African government in Rhodesia may some day have territorial ambitions towards Bechuanaland.

At the present political juncture, the white Government of Rhodesia, fully occupied after the break-up of the federation and resulting economic and political problems, is not actively interested in adventuring westwards. And across the border, neither the British Government nor the leaders of African political parties are interested in closer association with Southern Rhodesia. Thus, significant developments in the relationships of the two territories await a day when Africans have a greater voice in the affairs of Rhodesia.

Meanwhile, there is a key Bechuanaland issue involving Rhodesia. As we have already seen the only rail link between South Africa, its ports and land-locked Rhodesia passes through, and admirably serves, the eastern part of the

B.P. The northernmost extension of the South African Railways ends at Beit Bridge on the Transvaal–Rhodesian border. It is a short sixty-odd miles to the Rhodesian railhead at West Nicholson. In the past, Southern Rhodesia has been hesitant to see this link closed, despite repeated advances from the South African side, because of a fear by the English-speaking whites of Southern Rhodesia of being swallowed up economically by South Africa and, in later years, fear of a dynamic Afrikaner Nationalism. Not a few important figures in Rhodesian politics from 1948 to 1960 were English-speaking South Africans who had left the Republic. The whole climate has so changed in southern Africa that it is difficult to recall that from about 1948 to 1956 many people in South Africa either moved or bought farms in the Rhodesias as insurance against revolution in the former. Rhodesia had a clear and peaceful path of quiet multi-racial government, so the reasoning ran, and Afrikaner cabinet ministers were criticised by their own Press for buying farms in Northern and Southern Rhodesia as a precaution.

But the tide of African nationalism has swept down the continent, and not at the gentle snail's pace many sympathetic whites had not only welcomed but encouraged; the point has been reached where legislation against the African political parties in Rhodesia and the suspension of civil liberties are in some quarters felt to be more severe than in South Africa. Whites in Rhodesia are rather more fearful for their physical safety than their Republican counterparts, a fear reflected in a backtrek of significant numbers of whites who now feel that South Africa is the safer place for them. In the background of this is a process which tends to draw the white-dominated Government of Rhodesia closer to near-by South Africa (with fewer anti-South African leaders in the Rhodesian Press than were featured a decade ago) than appeared possible at the time the Federation was launched. Let us recall that it was the Labour Party in Great Britain, many of whose African experts wished to snatch Southern Rhodesia from the jaws of Afrikaner domination, who originally encouraged the Federation. Today, they would still fear Rhodesian ties with the Republic; however they no longer have any direct control of the situation. Far more important is the strong and sympathetic support of African leadership in independent Zambia and Malawi for the African political parties who oppose Southern white Government.

In the markedly changed climate of 1963, Southern Rhodesia and South Africa began secret discussions about establishing a direct rail link between the two countries. It is possible to go by rail from the Transvaal to Lourenço Marques in Mozambique, and thence on to Southern Rhodesia, but this is not a practicable route, nor politically safe if Portugal finds its hands full with an uprising in its east coast territory. The Mafeking-to-Bulawayo railway through Bechuanaland is vital.

So far, no responsible official of the B.P. Government nor any African leader has suggested that Bechuanaland could exert political pressure on either Rhodesia or South Africa by threatening to cut this link. Such a step is not likely at the present time. But in cold strategic logic, the possibility of such a cut stands out like a sore thumb. Trade between Rhodesia and South Africa is vital to both these countries. It would be a guerilla action of no great difficulty to cut the single line of rail—and to do it again when it had been repaired—despite genuine protective efforts of the Bechuanaland police. Both the potential threats—political and military—are real ones.

The discussions between Southern Rhodesia and South Africa were not, interestingly enough, primarily concerned with closing the short gap between West Nicholson and Beit Bridge. Building of this link is not the chief construction problem, which in fact occurs on the Rhodesia side of the border between West Nicholson and the main Rhodesian line. This section is lightly built, with many curves, and its improvement to a point where it would carry all South African–Rhodesian rail traffic would be difficult and expensive. A more likely route, currently under discussion, is from West Nicholson in the direction of the Rhodesian line to Lourenço Marques. Such a line would open up a fertile part of Rhodesia and would make a major development contribution. This line would provide much shorter access from the industrial parts of the Republic to the main centres of Rhodesia than does the present route whereby goods from Johannesburg destined for a Rhodesian station east of it on the map must first travel right across the Western Transvaal as part of an enormous loop.

Needless to say, people in authority in Bechuanaland are deeply concerned lest such a new railway be completed and deprive Bechuanaland of its excellent position in regard to train schedules. A future Government might, without the heavy through traffic, have to subsidise the railway in Bechuanaland. The British Ambassador in Pretoria is much concerned with the issue. So is Seretse Khama. He told me in late 1963 that he was prepared to go to Southern Rhodesia and personally appeal to the Government not to take a step which could have far-reaching and deleterious effects upon the economy of Bechuanaland.

Partly in order to meet Bechuanaland's anxiety, the territory signed an official agreement with Northern and Southern Rhodesia that both territories would consult the B.P. on any proposal relating to the railway which might adversely affect the traffic of the section passing through Bechuanaland. The Attorney General of Bechuanaland, A. G. Tilbury, also negotiated an agreement for consultation in the Railways Court set up by the two Rhodesias.

In the long run, as suggested in our consideration of Bechuanaland's ties with South West Africa, the long-held dream of making an Atlantic Coast outlet for Rhodesia could well be brought to fruition by crossing the Kalahari to a port in South West Africa or even, as has been mooted from time to time, utilising the superb potential harbour at the Bay of Tigers in southernmost Angola.

But at present the general conclusion must be that Bechuanaland and Rhodesia, despite their mutual boundary, have relatively little to say to each other.

Relations with Zambia (Northern Rhodesia)

An inherent difficulty of Bechuanaland following a really independent line *vis-à-vis* South Africa or, for its African leaders, *vis-à-vis* Great Britain, has been Bechuanaland's isolation from the fountainheads of Pan-Africanism. The African leaders of Bechuanaland, let alone the lesser lieutenants, have not until recently even met the men who mould African political thought. Seretse Khama did not meet Kenneth Kaunda, the Prime Minister of neighbouring Northern Rhodesia (Zambia), until both attended Kenya's independence celebration in Nairobi in December 1963. Time will certainly change this, but time will not alter the fact that Bechuanaland has come late and almost last to the ranks of emergent African countries. In addition to the late flowering of a sense of nationhood within its borders is the geographical isolation of Bechuanaland, without a seaport or a major airport. It is not easily accessible even to African leaders, many of whom could not pass through its neighbours.

The recent independence of Zambia at once makes leaders of Pan-Africa *persona grata* there. The pontoon ferry across the confluence of the Zambezi and the Chobe Rivers provides the physical access from Bechuanaland. Independent Zambia is in a position to offer economic assistance and, if it went that far, even military assistance or transit facilities for Bechuanaland-bound arms.

It is no reflection upon African states to say that the enthusiasm of the citizens of one country for providing major economic assistance to citizens of another has limits. The general unpopularity of Foreign Aid in the United States is matched by the once highly vocal criticism in

Ghana of the 'gift' of ten million pounds to Guinea announced in 1958. The fact that the amount was much larger than the development sum desperately requested by the relatively backward Northern Territory of Ghana, but turned down on grounds of financial stringency, left the Northerners something less than enchanted. The generosity and open-handed spirit of Dr. Kwame Nkrumah's practical demonstration of 'African brotherhood' foundered in part on the rock of Ghana nationalism, and the full sum is unlikely ever to be paid.

Zambia is probably richer *per capita* than any other independent African state. There is no doubt that the African leaders, judged by previous actions as well as by their solicited comments in Lusaka, will act with a spirit of brotherhood towards Bechuanaland and other poor African nations. But Zambia, for all its great copper revenues, has more worthwhile and needed projects for its own citizens than even it can finance. With the economic pressures stemming from the desires and aspirations of the masses—such as the demand that every child be given a chance to go to school in the country districts as well as in the urban areas—Zambia will very understandably think twice before subsidising another country. In the Pan-Africanist cause, the merit of a second front against the Portuguese in Angola's back door is itself to be weighed against Portuguese control of east and west coast ports.

In the short run, Zambia can now offer to Bechuanaland wise and sympathetic support, no doubt access to the new Zambian educational institutions, and also a strategic route for people as opposed to freight. In the long run, the possibilities of co-operation along both political and economic lines are however not numerous. Zambia can use only so much beef, and only some 7,000 carcasses now come annually from the B.P. The annual copper needs of the latter are less than the output of one mine for one day. But at least the two countries differ from many

African neighbours in that they do not compete for export markets.

Soviet Union and the United States

Without recapitulating their African policies in general, one can predict that both the great nuclear powers will approach Bechuanaland in accordance with past principles. Neither country is now actively concerned.

The United States policy of having its diplomatic reporting on Bechuanaland covered by occasional visitors from its Pretoria embassy makes economic sense, but has long been politically anachronistic. The U.S. was limited until 1964 to official relationships with Bechuanaland through appropriate British officials in London. The change to the present practice of stationing an American official in Swaziland to report on the three territories has merit but leaves the U.S. still isolated from daily contact with responsible leaders in Bechuanaland.

American policy is to keep its Peace Corps out of dependent countries, although the Peace Corps could provide a handful of desperately needed teachers for Bechuanaland. It is true that an exception to the dependency rule was made in the case of Nyasaland as a result of direct commitments by the late President Kennedy following approaches by Dr. Banda. It was of less consequence to the U.S. that the Federal Government of Rhodesia and Nyasaland was incensed by the way the Nyasaland Peace Corps project was handled than it was for the Americans to gain early good will among Nyasas. A similar premature start is unlikely in the High Commission Territories without open British approval.

The United States plays a part in a number of varied projects affecting Bechuanaland. Some Americans, particularly the historian, C. W. de Kiewiet, an American who grew up in South Africa, have played a significant role in the reorganisation of Roma College in Basutoland into a university for the three territories. 'Operation Crossroads', consisting of young Americans—white and Negro—has undertaken brief work projects in the B.P. American Metal Climax is involved through its control of Rhodesian Selection Trust and R.S.T's mineral agreement with the Bamangwato. The United States Navy operated a research project near Ghanzi during part of 1963. The American naval researchers set up a base in the far reaches of the Kalahari, because it is the one accessible point of land which is the exact antipodes of a radio station on American soil, and thus could be used to test the convergence of radio waves. But, on balance, the United States contact with Bechuanaland is minimal.

American concern with the power situation in southern Africa—over half of the American investments in Africa are in South Africa—and its traditional commitment to independence for colonial territories and encouragement of democratic government, suggests that the United States will keep a sharp eye on the territory of its closest N.A.T.O. ally. General support for British goals in Bechuanaland can be anticipated, as can eventual political and economic support of peaceful Bechuana aspirations.

The Soviet Union has even less direct contact with Bechuanaland, but it also keeping a weather eye on developments. Possibly the best informed Soviet academician is Professor Ivan Potekhin, long a specialist on southern Africa, although his only African field work has been in Ghana and Egypt. He is personally well aware of the basic facts of the Protectorate and, as he comments, is kept up to date by frequent visits to Moscow by people well informed on political developments in southern Africa.

The Soviet view of Bechuanaland was summarised in February 1963 by A. Strogovich in an article in the Moscow publication *Aziya i Afrika Segodnya* (*Asia and Africa Today*). The author strongly attacks the backwardness of the territory and lays this at the door of Great Britain. He criticises the expenditure of a quarter of the budget on the Administration and police compared with one-sixth on education and one-tenth on hospital services. The division of the country into 'tribal reservations' is attacked, as is the fact that Bechuanaland does not even have a paramount 'chief'. This comment should not be misunderstood as supporting chiefs, since the appointment of chiefs is criticised as being backward. The Soviet article regrets the lack of an organisation to 'combine the efforts of the whole people against the enslavers . . .', inasmuch as 'every effort to establish such an organisation met with punishment of the workers'. At the time of the article, Soviet praise was highest for the B.P.P. and its President Motsete and (then) General Secretary Mpho.

The Soviet reaction to Prime Minister Verwoerd's overture to the inhabitants of the High Commission Territories, to judge by *Pravda* (18 December 1963), was to imply that Britain was falsely building up South Africa as a threat in order to frighten Africans. They would then prefer to remain as 'colonial slaves' rather than be part of Dr. Verwoerd's 'concentration camps'.

The Soviet mistake described earlier of receiving Mr. Matante of the B.P.P. in Moscow, when they expected a woman of the same name, is not an indication of lack of interest, nor necessarily of poor organisation, but rather of the difficulty of operating so many thousands of miles away from one's nearest diplomatic base. Soviet theory regarding workers and peasants in West Africa has undergone considerable modification with experience. The expulsion of the highly regarded Soviet ambassador to Guinea, their unpublicised gaffe in refusing a visa to a touring Ugandan ambassador, and many other mistakes, suggest that Soviet efforts in southern Africa will be as much by the trial and error method as those of most nations inexperienced in a new region.

Although the Communist Party operates freely in Basutoland, and has recently begun publication of the Party publication TOKOLOKO (Freedom), there is no legal Communist Party in Bechuanaland. It is doubtful if a genuine *sub-rosa* party exists. A few individual Bechuanas who have lived in South Africa are to one degree or another Marxist-oriented, but they are not bound together in an active organisation.

Since the decision of the Communist Party in South Africa to undertake active sabotage, a substantial number of well-known and thus exposed Party members have passed through Bechuanaland from the Republic, en route to points north.

Great publicity was given in 1963 to the escape via Swaziland into Bechuanaland by Harold Wolpe and Arnold Goldreich, who had been arrested following the Rivonia Raid near Johannesburg, in which short-wave equipment and incriminating evidence was reported to have been found by the police. Among the latter there was said to have been a paper on the manufacture of incendiary bombs in Goldreich's handwriting. Both Wolpe and Goldreich were extremely nervous while in Francistown, and voluntarily spent several nights in jail. There was certainly hostility among the white population. When the DC-3 sent by East African Airways was sabotaged and burned on the Francistown airport, the nervousness increased. Most observers believe that it was the local act of a group of white residents without the knowledge of the Bechuanaland police and without assistance from South African sources. However, no definite evidence is available to confirm or deny this theory.

So far, the Soviet Union has not extended itself on the tactical level in southern Africa. Trade with South Africa continues both through intermediaries and directly as far as diamonds are concerned. The involvement in Bechuanaland of any local Communists appears to be characteristic of unassisted efforts, such as those the Communist Party in South Africa has struggled for decades to mount and finance without material assistance from the Communist world. The potential challenge to the Soviet Union by Peking for control of the Communist movements in southern

Africa could change this rapidly. One possible portent is the headway made by the Cape Town-based pro-Peking Y.C.C.C. (Yu Chi Chan Club), believed to have been led by Neville Alexander before his imprisonment, concentrating upon the Coloured population, as distinct from the Muscovite Communist efforts to influence Africans by penetration and manipulation of the African National Congress.

One may assume a general rise in both Soviet and American interest in Bechuanaland. The intensity of concern may, like that in Africa generally, vary inversely with the extension of more cordial feelings between the Cold War leaders. The amount of trade involved is not significant to either power. The politically strategic value of the Protectorate is the key to actions in Washington or Moscow.

Pan-African Movement

Pan-Africanism has many forms. Culturally, Africans of the French expression, particularly in Senegal, have given the lead. President Kwame Nkrumah of Ghana has contributed ideas of an 'African personality'. Economically, the African states seek to raise their living standards by co-operation in trade and development. Politically, the emergence from the Addis Ababa Conference of a unitary organisation of African states was a major boost. Militarily, the movement seeks the elimination of colonialism from the continent, and particularly the end of Portuguese and white South African rule. The military objective is a major contributor to political unity.

Both African parties in Bechuanaland are sympathetic to the cultural, economic, and political goals of Pan-Africanism. Neither would support the laws of Angola or of South Africa. But the Bechuanaland Democratic Party is less willing to achieve military goals at the price of sacrificing economic goals, and possibly bringing about the disintegration of Bechuanaland itself.

Some general guidelines applicable to Bechuanaland were laid down by the Co-ordinating Committee of the African organisation. These were first successfully applied by the Goodwill Mission of the Co-ordinating Committee for the Liberation of Africa to the Angola Nationalists in Leopoldville from 13 to 18 July 1963. The eight general principles include three which apply particularly to Bechuanaland:

In considering aid to any given colonial or dependent territory, the dependent territory, the relation, concern and interest of immediate neighbouring independent African countries with contiguous boundaries must be taken into consideration as well.

Independent countries geographically contiguous to a given non-independent country because of their local knowledge and proximity, should play a vital role in the advancement and progress of that territory to the goal of liberation and independence.

Where an independent state is used as a base for the purpose of liberation of a colonial territory care must be taken to evolve such a policy of action as would not lead to the destruction of sovereignty and independence of that State or prejudicing its security.

Another general principle is the avoidance of competing organisations. This is meant to force a common front inside a country under pressure. Whether it applies to Bechuanaland in relation to its neighbours is doubtful. In the heyday of the Casablanca group, Ghana had taken the lead by supporting the Bechuanaland People's Party. However, before the Addis Ababa Conference, Ghanaian support (in total less than £1,000) had dwindled. Whether the new organisation would support one African party against another in Bechuanaland is as doubtful as whether it would apply pressure to make them merge. Much depends upon whether the B.P. is itself viewed as a country to 'fight for', or primarily in the light of its physical proximity to South Africa, South West Africa, Rhodesia, and even Angola.

During 1963, the Pan-African nations were successful in promoting a recommendation to the General Assembly by the United Nations Special Committee on Colonialism to send U.N. observer teams to the High Commission Territories to prevent a South African 'take-over'. The vote was adopted by 17 to 3, with 2 abstentions. Britain, Australia, and the United States formed the negative minority. This recommendation did not lead to action, although another part of it, urging Britain to proceed to general elections based upon universal suffrage, will soon be acted upon. It is however likely that this British action was not significantly affected by this particular U.N. Committee recommendation.

Relations with Great Britain

Not only does Great Britain administer Bechuanaland, provide many of its public servants, and protect it in the larger world, but Britain is likely to be the closest of all nations to an independent Bechuanaland. African experience suggests that for most former British, French, and Belgian colonies, the tie with the metropolitan power remains close even where the acid of war, as in Algeria, or the acidity of being rejected, as France was by Guinea, corrodes their history. There is virtually no genuine antagonism against Great Britain among the Bechuanas. There are many unsatisfied wants, historical instances of misjudgments, inequities, and, always, the anti-colonial cry which precedes independence. But when one questions the leaders and rank and file of the more militant Bechuanaland People's Party, their grievances have a petty ring to them, and they are ready to break off a denunciation of Britain to have tea with one of Her Majesty's officials.

The power relationships of the U.K. to the Protectorate are closely interwoven with Britain's policies towards South Africa, a subject calling for a lengthy book in itself. When you have over one thousand million pounds invested in a country, approximately a quarter of your overseas investments, there is reason to weigh words with care. Other British concerns are affected by the strategic importance of the Cape of Good Hope and the Simonstown naval base, the position of all three territories, and, despite the severance of Commonwealth association, an extra-legal tie to over one million British-descended citizens of the Republic of South Africa. Also in the scale, and weighing more heavily with passing years, are the wishes and interests of the Commonwealth, and especially India, Pakistan and the new African members. Neither Great Britain nor the United States was happy to find itself as part of small and thoroughly out-voted minorities on many of the key African issues at the United Nations in 1963.

If Britain is occasionally under siege for persevering with certain principles which may involve an unpopular position *vis-à-vis* either South Africa or Rhodesia, she has little hesitation in implementing the various liberal provisions of the United Nations Charter in Bechuanaland itself. The local Administration is forthrightly opposed to discrimination on the basis of race, and many of its members make a particular effort in their personal lives to give extra help to individual Bechuanas.

Special mention must be made of the Abrahams kidnapping case to which Dr. Verwoerd referred in his major policy statement. It is an example of Britain standing up strongly for what was right in Bechuanaland on one hand, but not giving way to panic and hasty and ill-advised action on the other. Dr. Kenneth Abrahams is a South African, classified as Coloured, and a graduate of the University of Cape Town Medical School. According to friends of his whom I interviewed, he was never very politically minded. That is often a matter of degree among educated Coloured people in Cape Town, because even those who are known as 'pro-Government' are rarely in sympathy with many aspects of the traditional segregation in South Africa, and have been further irritated by petty *'klein apartheid'* annoyances in recent years.

Be that as it may, the South African Police sought to arrest Dr. Abrahams in the Baster area of Rehoboth, south of Windhoek in South West Africa. The Basters resisted the idea of arresting their doctor (and political mentor?) and refused to co-operate. A four-hour community meeting issued a statement that 'every man, woman and child will surround the house and the only way the police can take him away is over our dead bodies.'

The Rehoboth Basters are a proud, stubborn, suspicious people. Their origins lie in the eighteenth century Cape Colony when, as a racially mixed group descended from Boer farmers and Hottentots, they trekked north to establish their own republic. Like similar republics of that era, they considered themselves proper 'burghers', and to this day take great pride in their individual land ownership. Many of them are light complexioned, and on the whole they do not associate with either the usual Cape Coloured population or any of the African groups. The South African Government has found them very prickly to deal with as a community. Its attempt in the Odendaal Report to create a 'Basterstan' has had a mixed reception.

Behind the scenes, their show of resistance to the group of policemen and security officers in Rehoboth escalated rapidly to the highest level of the South African Government. Quite unusually, the South African Government did not force the issue in the light of the extremely delicate nature of South West Africa's political status. Sufficient evidence appears to have been available (later related to material the South African Police say was uncovered in the Rivonia raid) for Dr. Abrahams' arrest under South African law. However, the police stalled their action and finally, on 18 July 1963, the Deputy Minister of South West African Affairs announced that Abrahams would not be arrested, provided he did not leave the Baster capital and concentrated on his medical work.

Two weeks later, on 3 August, it was reported that Dr.
Abrahams, with two companions, had secretly left the settlement, succeeded in avoiding police posts, and had passed
into western Bechuanaland. Early on the morning of 11
August, some miles out of Ghanzi on the road to Lobatsi,
they were held up in 'wild west' fashion by six men. Some
were armed, wore masks, blue jeans, cowboy hats and
revolver holsters. Abrahams and his companions were then
kidnapped after a scuffle and taken back to South West
Africa.

On 14 August the South African Commissioner of Police
announced that Abrahams had been arrested by a police
patrol in the Gobabis District (adjoining Bechuanaland)
and was already in Cape Town to be charged with violation
of the Suppression of Communism Act and the act against
sabotage.

The South African Minister of Justice, John Vorster,
who generally speaks with legal caution, made a statement
in which he branded as ridiculous the subsequent charge
that the South African Police had anything to do with
the kidnapping. He had every logical reason to make such a
statement. Presumably, he knew nothing of any kidnapping
plans. The Prime Minister had said repeatedly that South
Africa had to use great tolerance in dealing with the
Territories. If the Minister of Justice was already refrain-
ing from arresting a man inside South West Africa, why
risk the easily exposed and diplomatically dangerous action
of kidnapping a man in British territory? Obviously, the
Minister could not believe that an individual policeman
could act so foolishly on his own responsibility.

Not all the true facts have ever emerged. What appears
to have happened is that an over-zealous South African
policeman, with assistance from local farmers, took it upon
himself to make up for Abrahams slipping through the
police posts. Indeed, one farmer apparently believed that
if he could talk to the men from South West Africa, his

racial good will would lead them to remain in South West of their own volition.

The South African courts, when they have jurisdiction, can be very jealous of correct legal procedure. Far more often than the world recognises, they are a thorn in the side of Government prosecutors. When Dr. Abrahams was brought to the Cape Town courtroom, it was crowded with Coloured friends, interested Africans, and Europeans. In the gallery, they were all jammed together, sitting and standing in a friendly fashion prohibited in the southern states of America.

Abrahams' lawyer was Advocate Benjamin Kies, a Coloured former teacher often in conflict with segregation laws. His opponent was a highly promising young Afrikaner advocate, Jan Steyn. The Chief Justice could scarcely have been more sympathetic to Kies as he presented his argument. The Government had no case at all. Steyn soon admitted this and conceded all Kies' argument in advance. But Kies was arguing not only for Abrahams' release, but to make political capital against the Government. He asked numerous embarrassing questions about where warrants were sworn, where the prisoner was arrested, and which police were involved. Finally, a judge asked Kies whether or not he really wanted his client to be free or, the judge implied, carry on the case. Dr. Abrahams was released shortly thereafter and joined his wife in Bechuanaland. The actions of the South African authorities were partly a response to court evidence, but Abrahams could have been rearrested on charges which would not come before the court. His release reflected South Africa's desire for good relations with Bechuanaland.

But it was also an issue on which Britain could not compromise. Nevertheless, the British authorities in Bechuanaland did not fill the air with accusations and thus make it all the harder for South Africa to acknowledge error. For once, justice prevailed *sotto voce*.

CONCLUSION

Three major pre-independence issues facing Bechuanaland emerge from observations we have already made.
The first of these is that the rapid strides towards a sense of
nationhood must continue if a nation it is to be. Tribalism
is a potent force, if less violent because of the ethnic closeness
of the Bechuana tribes; the apparent reluctance of some
tribal groupings and some chiefs to pool resources in the
national interest could however be critical. If they do not
sink their differences, they will sink their country.

The two main parties are not dangerously far apart in
their political goals. Coalition is feasible. At present, if
either major party won an election, neither would feel a
need to imprison the leaders of their opposition. So far,
Bechuanaland has sailed in the lee of Great Britain and has
yet to feel the full force of the Macmillan 'wind of change'.
When and if outside forces begin backing one or another
party or faction inside Bechuanaland, dangerous rifts
may develop with an exacerbation of tribal feelings and the
threat of civil war. Concurrently, one must stress that
relationships among tribes, and also between Africans and
Europeans, have for decades been without organised ill-
feeling and without violence. Unless this calm continues,
the slim reed of Bechuana nationalism will be buffeted by
cruel winds before it has taken deep root.

The second pre-independence need, expanded economic
development, has been stressed along with the desirability
of diversification and the opening of new sources of national
revenue. The necessity for close economic ties with South
Africa or a carefully thought out substitute for them is
critical. The contributions of white South Africans, many of
whom are among the strongest boosters of an independent
nation within the B.P., will become even more necessary.
Indeed, as one of the B.P. officials most concerned with
development has observed 'Bechuanaland can still fall
back on an essentially subsistence economy; but the time is

approaching when the dependence upon the Republic will
be crucial.'

The third issue is the whole arena of the formal and legal
development of Bechuanaland and its external relations.
Britain is as unlikely to cast adrift a ship of state headed
for a political reef as a ship with an economically leaky hull.
A recurring theme of these pages is that buckets of economic
help will not fill political sieves. It is on the political side
that Bechuana leaders must provide their own answers.

Lord Hailey concludes his recent study of relationships
between South Africa and the territories by advising the
territories that 'It would be well for them to realise that
liberties once lost are not easily regained by the small
peoples of the world. What would it profit the small peoples
of the Territories if they now loose their hold on the solid
fact of liberty under British rule, in order that they may
grasp at the fantasy of Independence?'

From another perspective, we would place less emphasis
for the future on bilateral relationships between Bechuanaland and Britain and greater emphasis than does Lord
Hailey on three other factors: the ability of Bechuanas to
steer their ship of state successfully with less help from their
colonial mentor; the greater influence on Bechuanaland
from the Organisation of African Unity and their greater
influence in the United Nations in protecting the interest
of Bechuanaland from possible encroachment; and, finally,
a much more malleable South African policy, one not
without elements of genuine friendship on South Africa's
part.

Many issues posed by the alternatives of our title—
Bechuanaland: Pan-African Outpost or Bantu Homeland?
—have been ventilated in what we hope is a frank discussion. Time will obviously write the final answer to the
question. Of the strategic nature of Bechuanaland in the
struggle between Pan-Africanism and the Bantustan
concept we have little doubt. But one factor we hope has
emerged from these pages is a feeling for Bechuanaland and

the Bechuanas as not either belonging to South Africa's cause or existing solely to serve a Pan-Africanist cause, but as a modern Bechuana nation to take its place among the sovereign states of African or freely to decide to associate itself in some larger political entity which will allow full expression to the Bechuanas. If history has not been altogether kind to them, neither has she written her worst pages about them. Let their future be for the Bechuanas to write.

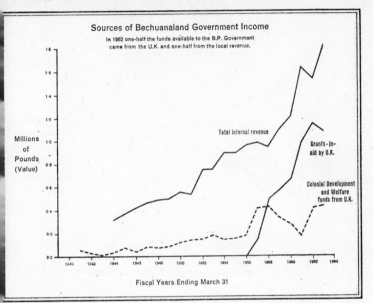

Sources of Bechuanaland Government Income

In 1962 one-half the funds available to the B.P. Government came from the U.K. and one-half from the local revenue.

Millions of Pounds (Value)

Total internal revenue

Grants-in-aid by U.K.

Colonial Development and Welfare funds from U.K.

Fiscal Years Ending March 31

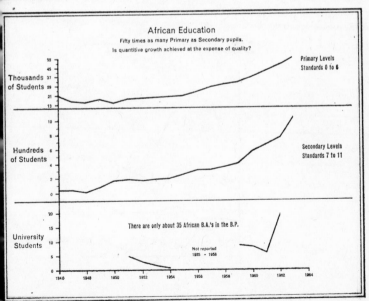

African Education

Fifty times as many Primary as Secondary pupils.
Is quantitive growth achieved at the expense of quality?

Thousands of Students

Primary Levels Standards 0 to 6

Hundreds of Students

Secondary Levels Standards 7 to 11

University Students

There are only about 35 African B.A.'s in the B.P.

Not reported 1955 - 1958

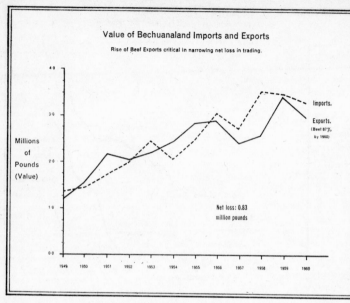

Value of Bechuanaland Imports and Exports

Rise of Beef Exports critical in narrowing net loss in trading.

Imports.

Exports.
(Beef 87%,
by 1960)

Millions
of
Pounds
(Value)

Net loss: 0.83
million pounds

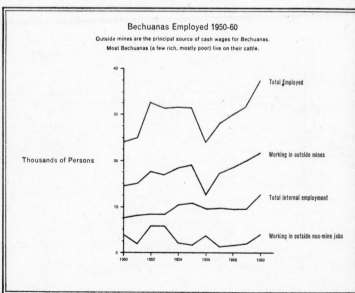

Bechuanas Employed 1950-60

Outside mines are the principal source of cash wages for Bechuanas.
Most Bechuanas (a few rich, mostly poor) live on their cattle.

Thousands of Persons

Total Employed

Working in outside mines

Total internal employment

Working in outside non-mine jobs

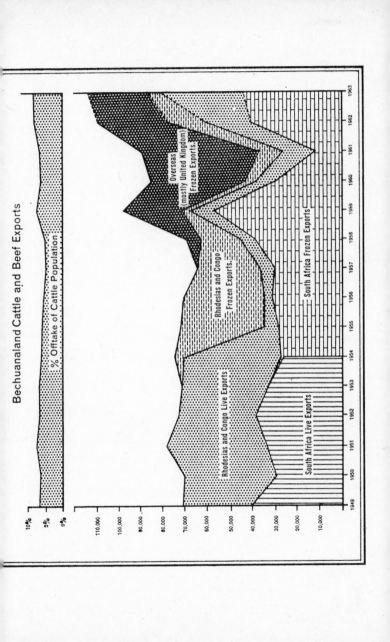

Bechuanaland Cattle and Beef Exports